A NORTON
POCKET GUIDE
to Grammar and
Punctuation

Dawn Rodrigues

MASSACHUSETTS COLLEGE OF LIBERAL ARTS

Myron Tuman

NICHOLLS STATE UNIVERSITY

W. W. NORTON & COMPANY

New York • London

W. W. Norton & Company has been independent since its founding in 1923, when William Warder Norton and Mary D. Herter Norton first published lectures delivered at the People's Institute, the adult education division of New York City's Cooper Union. The Nortons soon expanded their program beyond the Institute, publishing books by celebrated academics from America and abroad. By mid-century, the two major pillars of Norton's publishing program—trade books and college texts—were firmly established. In the 1950s, the Norton family transferred control of the company to its employees, and today—with a staff of four hundred and a comparable number of trade, college, and professional titles published each year—W. W. Norton & Company stands as the largest and oldest publishing house owned wholly by its employees.

The text of this book is composed in ITC Stone Serif and Helvetica
with the display set in Rockwell.
Composition by Binghamton Valley Composition.

ISBN 0-393-92937-X
ISBN 13: 978-0-393-92937-9

W. W. Norton & Company, Inc., 500 Fifth Avenue, New York NY 10110-0017
www.wwnorton.com
W. W. Norton & Company Ltd., Castle House, 75/76 Wells Street, London
W1T 3QT

2 3 4 5 6 7 8 9 0

HOW TO USE THIS BOOK

A Norton Pocket Guide to Grammar and Punctuation is designed so that you can use it easily on your own, to find the information you need as you write. Here are some of the ways you can find what you're looking for in the book:

A Brief Contents on the inside front cover lists all the chapters in the book. If you know the general topic you're looking for—commas, for example—this is the place to start.

A Detailed Contents on the inside back cover lists both chapters and the headings within each chapter. If you are looking for help with a specific issue—using commas between items in a series, for example—start here.

The Index lists everything that is covered in this book. You can find what you need by looking up a general topic (articles) or, if you do not know what the topic is called, by looking up specific words (*a, an*).

Checklists offer help with issues that writers often stumble over—fixing comma splices, editing out wordiness, making sentences parallel, and so on. You'll find these checklists throughout the book in blue boxes.

A Glossary of Usage in Chapter 5 provides brief advice on commonly confused words—*a* and *an, lay* and *lie, principal* and *principle*, and so on.

Examples provide models that demonstrate how to write grammatically and appropriately. We've made the examples easy to spot by putting a little green pointer to the left of each one. Notice that many of the examples in this book are hand-edited, so that you can see common errors and how to edit them at a glance.

Sentences
and Words

1 Effective Sentences

Effective sentence structure can help you improve the over-all style of your writing and communicate your meaning clearly. Keep in mind, however, that the purpose of your writing task and the specific focus of each paragraph should affect your choice of words and the structure of your sentences. One good rule to keep in mind is that, in general, English sentences work like relay teams in track: they perform best with the strongest material at the end. For example, if you are assigned an essay on study habits, you should write: "So that you can be admitted into the college of your choice, study hard." On the other hand, if your essay focuses on getting into the college of your choice, you should write: "Study hard so you will be admitted into the college of your choice."

1a Active and Passive Voices

In the active voice, the subject acts; in the passive voice, the subject is acted upon. Use active verbs unless you have a reason to do otherwise. Reserve the passive for specific purposes: to de-emphasize the agent or doer of the action or to create greater coherence between sentences.

ACTIVE VOICE   When possible, use the active voice, with subjects acting on objects.

> ▶ The judge dismissed the charges against the students.

The subject of the sentence, "judge," is doing the acting.

PASSIVE VOICE   Passive verbs are constructed by combining a form of *to be* and the past-participle form of the verb. When converting a sentence from passive to active, ask yourself who or what acted, and then use your answer as the subject of the sentence. Consider the following:

► The charges against one of the students were dismissed by the judge.

To determine how to transform this sentence, ask, "Who dismissed the charges?" Your answer produces the following active sentence: "The judge dismissed the charges against one of the students."

Sometimes you may *choose* to use the passive voice. You may want to draw attention to or away from the subject.

► Millions died in the Auschwitz concentration camp. They were remembered by survivors during a recent memorial service.

The first sentence in the above example focuses on "millions" who died and is in the active voice. The second sentence, which is in the passive voice, begins with "they"—a pronoun reference to "millions"—and links the second sentence with the first. In this case, using the passive helps the writer create coherence between sentences.

1b   Parallel Construction

Use parallel construction to show the relationships among similar ideas. In the following sentences, the balance of elements heightens the effect of the ideas being conveyed.

► Do not ask what your country can do for you. Ask what you can do for your country.

► A nation of the people, for the people, and by the people shall not perish from the earth.

Avoid faulty parallelism—the failure to put similar items into similar grammatical structures. The writer should revise the following sentences to create parallel structure.

► To raise extra revenue, colleges often write grants, conduct fund-raising drives, and ~~alumni are often asked to contribute~~ solicit contributions from alumni .

► Some of my hobbies are running track, traveling, and playing volleyball.

CHECKLIST 1

Using Parallel Sentence Structure

- Use repetition to pair ideas.
    - ▶ Give me liberty or give me death.
- Make sure all items in a series are presented in the same grammatical form.
    - ▶ People select foreign cars for their value, ~~they perform well~~ , *their performance* and their style.
- Use coordinating conjunctions (*and, but, for, nor, or, so, yet*) to link and balance parallel ideas. The sentence logic and your purpose as a writer should determine your choice of connecting words.
    - ▶ The federal government is giving more power to states and local municipalities *and* taking away power from national agencies.

    And signals an additive relationship and indicates that you see both actions as equally important.

    - ▶ The federal government is giving more power to states, *but* it is taking away money from social services agencies nationally.

    But signals a trade-off.
- Use pairs of correlative conjunctions (*either . . . or; neither . . . nor; not only . . . but also*) to link clauses.
    - ▶ *Neither* my mother *nor* my brother would help me paint my apartment.

1c   Coordination and Subordination

Use coordination and subordination to help your reader understand the relationship between ideas in your writing. Coordination refers to the use of coordinate conjunctions (*and, but, for, nor, or, so, yet*) to link parts of sentences. Subordination refers to placing ideas of lesser importance in subordinate (dependent) clauses and placing more important ideas in the main clause.

By deciding which ideas should be subordinated and then selecting the approriate subordinating conjunctions—the words that connect the ideas—you can help readers understand how different ideas relate to one another. Subordinating conjunctions such as the following are used in subordination: *after, although, as, as if, as though, because, before, even though, if, since, so that, than, that, though, unless, until, when, where, whereas, while.*

Although subordination can strengthen your writing, excessive subordination can ruin it. If your sentences go on and on, try shortening them by combining sentences or by deleting unnecessary uses of *that* and *which.*

Use subordinate clauses carefully, making sure that you express ideas or concepts appropriately.

▶ They stopped for lunch and spent time talking.

In the above example, the clauses express concepts that match; therefore, coordination is effective. In the example below, the clauses in the unrevised sentence do not appear to match. The subordinate conjunction *after* gives the reader an indication of the relationship between the clauses in this sentence.

▶ They went shopping, and then they talked about the current state of the economy in Japan and Korea.

REVISED   After they went shopping, they talked about the current state of the economy in Japan and Korea.

If your writing has many short, choppy sentences, you may need to combine some of those sentences, using either coordination or subordination. By selecting an appropriate subordinator, you have a chance to reconsider your meaning in the sentences, and your revision may be significantly different from your original sentence.

▶ The World Wide Web has attracted many kinds of people. It attracts small business owners. Students use it, too. Government agencies provide access to their forms.

REVISED   Because the World Wide Web is so versatile, it has attracted a range of people, including small business owners, students, and government officials.

1d Wordy Sentences

Wordy sentences can obscure your meaning. Aim for clear, direct sentences so readers can follow your ideas.

1. Substitute appositives (words that mean the same thing as the word to which they refer) for clauses beginning with *who* or *which.*

Using Coordination and Subordination

- Combine equally important short sentences by using appropriate coordinating conjunctions.

  ▶ Passengers can visit the island at their leisure. If they want, they can remain on board.

  REVISED Passengers can either visit the island at their leisure or remain on board.

- Reduce less important sentences to phrases or dependent clauses, and combine them with the main clause by using subordinating conjunctions.

  ▶ I worked on the project all night long. But I knew our group would fail.

  REVISED I worked on the project all night long even though I knew our group would fail.

- Remove unnecessary, repetitive words between sentences.

  ▶ Beekeepers use a centrifuge. The centrifuge is used to extract honey that comes from a comb.

  REVISED Beekeepers use centrifuges to extract honey that comes from combs.

- Reduce less important sentences or clauses to phrases, using -ing or -ed words at the beginning or end of a sentence.

  ▶ She has become bored by routine tax-law work. She hopes to become a defense attorney.

  REVISED Bored by routine tax law, she hopes to become a defense attorney.

  ▶ Mr. Stevens, ~~who was~~ my former neighbor, won his lawsuit.

2. Delete expletives (words such as *it is, here is,* and *there is* that are added to a sentence without adding to the meaning of the sentence).

  ▶ ~~There is~~ a chatroom on the Web called Study Hall ~~that~~ encourages students to talk with one another about college courses.

3. Use modifiers instead of prepositional and verbal phrases.

   ▶ He carries a leather briefcase ~~made out of leather~~.

   ▶ He carries a weather-beaten leather briefcase ~~made out of leather that is weather-beaten~~.

   Note: **Compound modifiers** (modifiers made up of more than one word, such as "weather-beaten" in the example above) are often hyphenated.

4. Eliminate unnecessary words, choosing simple one-word expressions rather than longer phrases (see Checklist 3, below).

   ▶ The company is taking applications now ~~at this point in time~~.

1e Sentence Variety

Different situations call for different kinds of sentences. News stories, for example, usually contain relatively short, simple sentences, whereas editorials and feature stories include longer, more complex sentences. In all cases, good writing is characterized by variety in sentence structure. Variety height-

Replacing Wordy Expressions with One-Word Substitutes — CHECKLIST 3

INSTEAD OF	USE
at this point in time	now
because of the fact that	because
be of the opinion that	think
during the same time that	when
has the ability to	can
in spite of the fact that	although
in today's world	today
red in color	red
until such time as	until

ens interest and allows writers to create an effect that is well suited to the meaning of their text. Consider the following sentences:

> ▶ Another border patrol agent was fired at today by several suspected drug dealers. The suspects escaped.

The second, short sentence of this news report emphasizes that the suspects got away.

> ▶ Instead of devoting so much attention to protecting the rights of illegal immigrants, we need to consider the dangers being faced daily by the border patrol agents, many of whom are new to this area and far away from family and relatives. Border patrol agents work long hours, protect our downtown streets, and return the next day to face the same dangers all over again. We appreciate their hard work and compliment them for their heroic effort. Their efforts this past year have reduced illegal immigration by more than 50 percent over previous years. They deserve our praise and our support.

The variety in this example, from an editorial, illustrates that well-crafted, long sentences are often easier to follow than shorter sentences, for they demonstrate clear relationships between ideas.

A PERSONAL LIBRARY OF EFFECTIVE SENTENCE PATTERNS
Keep an eye out for particularly well-crafted sentences. When you see them, jot them down or store them in a computer file. While drafting or revising an assignment, refer to the file, and consider imitating sentences that might help you to communicate your thoughts better.

2 Errors in Sentence Wording

2a Misplaced Modifiers

Modifiers are words, phrases, or clauses that describe other words, phrases, or clauses. Modifiers are misplaced if readers are unable to determine what the modifiers describe or explain. To correct a sentence with a misplaced modifier, either move the modifier to a new position or rewrite the sentence.

> ▶ Marching across the field, the band played the fight song ~~rang out~~ for all to hear.

The band, not the fight song, is doing the marching.

a business person must spend at

▶ To be successful ~~in business~~, long hours ~~of~~ work ~~are required~~.

Placing the words "long hours" next to "business" implies that long hours, not a person, are doing the working.

While walking home,

▶ Randall found a twenty-dollar bill ~~walking home~~.

Randall, not the twenty-dollar bill, was walking home.

MISPLACED LIMITING MODIFIERS Limiting modifiers are words that restrict or limit the meaning of the word or word group they modify. Place limiting modifiers *almost, even, exactly, hardly, just, merely, nearly, only, scarcely,* and *simply* in front of the word or words you wish to modify. Be sure to create the precise effect you want to have on your reader.

▶ We must *only* go as far as the next town.

The writer is saying that going to the next town is all that we've got to do. The focus is on what has to be done—only going as far as the next town.

▶ We must go *only* as far as the next town.

The writer is focusing on how far we have to go—only to the next town.

▶ The instructor did not *even* call me once.

The writer is focusing on the fact that the instructor not only didn't do other things, he/she didn't even call her.

▶ The instructor did not call me *even* once.

The writer focuses only on the act of calling, noting that the instructor didn't do it even one time.

SQUINTING MODIFIERS A modifier that could refer to the preceding or following words is said to squint. Be sure to place modifiers where the reference is clear. Try moving phrases around so that your meaning is unambiguous.

Before noon, he

▶ ~~He~~ said ~~before noon~~ he'd be here.

In the unrevised sentence above, "before noon" could refer to either "He said" or "he'd be here."

DANGLING MODIFIERS Modifiers are said to be dangling when they fail to modify logically any word or words in a sentence. To correct a dangling modifier, ask who or what is responsible for the action described in the opening word group. Immediately after the *-ing* word group, name that person or thing. You may need to rewrite the sentence.

▶ Before going on vacation, the bills ~~need to be paid~~. *I need to pay*

▶ After cutting the grass, the garden ~~was weeded~~. *I weeded*

▶ ~~Traveling~~ for four weeks, ~~returning~~ to work ~~was a burden~~. *After traveling he found it difficult to return*

2b   Split Infinitives

An infinitive consists of *to* and a verb or verb phrase—for example, *to write*, *to swim well*, *to act quickly*. An infinitive is said to be **split** when a word or words appear between its two parts, as in *to gladly serve*. Infinitives can be split in informal writing, but in college writing and other more formal situations, reword sentences that contain split infinitives. Check with your professor or your employer if you want to be sure of expectations.

▶ To ~~properly~~ care for your plants, you need to repot them regularly. *properly*

"Properly" modifies the infinitive "to care."

2c   Shifts in Construction

Some sentence problems seem accidental and are thus hard to label. This section covers errors that result when a writer in advertently makes any shift: a shift away from topics in the subject of the sentence; a shift in tense; a shift in pronoun person and number; and a shift from statements to commands or from statements to wishes, often called shifts in mood.

SHIFT FROM SUBJECT TO PREDICATE   When you start an idea in the subject part of a sentence, you must complete that idea—not another idea—in the predicate. To correct sentences that end up differently from the way they started, you may need to reconsider completely the point you want to make.

▶ ~~When I bake~~ cookies relaxes me. *Baking*

or

▶ ~~When~~ I bake cookies ~~relaxes me~~. *I relax when*

In the first revision, the subject matches the predicate. In the second revision, the predicate completes the sentence structure implied by the subject.

> *I was appointed*
> ▶ ~~My appointment to~~ Director ' ~~was~~ the position I wanted.
>   ^   ^

The revised version makes distinct the two ideas in the sentence: the appointment and the writer's note that she wanted the job.

SHIFT IN TENSE   The verb tense used in a sentence should give readers a clear idea of the *time* of the action described. Be consistent in using verb tense, shifting tenses only as required. An abrupt shift in tense can confuse readers.

> *are*
> ▶ Workers who ~~were~~ consulted regularly feel more committed to
>   ^
>   *have*
>   the company and ~~had~~ a lower rate of absenteeism.
>   ^

or

> *have been*   *now*
> ▶ Workers who ~~were~~ consulted regularly feel more committed to
>   ^   ^
>
>   the company and have a lower rate of absenteeism.

The original sentence refers to an action in the past ("workers were consulted"), then switches to the present ("regularly feel"), then moves back to the past "had a lower rate"). To revise a sentence with faulty predication, you must clarify your intent as a writer.

As a rule, use the present tense when referring to the actions of literary characters.

> *delays*   *is*
> ▶ Hamlet ~~delayed~~ because he ~~was~~ overwhelmed by the events
>   ^   ^
>
>   of the past few days.

SHIFT IN PRONOUN PERSON AND NUMBER   Pronoun references should be consistent throughout a paper. That is, if you start writing from one point of view, do not shift to another. If you are writing about yourself, then maintain an *I* point of view throughout the paper.

> ▶ My summer internships gave me the opportunity to observe different business settings. I discovered that I like working for a faster-paced company, one in which workers rarely leave before 6 P.M.

If you are addressing the reader directly, maintain a "your" point of view.

▶ Go to the first stop sign, then turn right. After traveling for three blocks, watch for a bridge.

If you start writing a paper in the third person (using pronouns such as *he*, *she*, *it*, or *they* and synonyms such as *a person*, *a platypus*, *students*, and *tourists*), a shift to *I* may be appropriate, but not a shift to *you*.

▶ Characters in each of these stories were driven to express their
creativity. ~~You~~ can't help but wonder whether the woman in
  ^I
"The Yellow Wallpaper" would have recovered if she had been
allowed to write.

Note: Although many teachers now recognize that *I* and *you* are used in many writing situations, including some academic publications, some teachers still oppose the use of *I* or *you* in college papers. Remember that it is possible, and often better, to state your opinions without using *I*. If you are uncertain about using *I* or *you*, check with your instructor.

   Affirmative
▶ ~~I personally feel that affirmative~~ action is not fair to minorities.
   ^

In an opinion essay, your readers recognize that the statements you make are your "personal feelings." You do not have to use the words "I personally feel" or "I think."

SHIFT FROM STATEMENTS TO COMMANDS (SHIFT IN MOOD)
A shift in mood refers to a shift in the approach to a topic. In the indicative mood, ideas are expressed matter-of-factly.

▶ Your room needs to be cleaned.

The imperative mood is characterized by commands or requests.

▶ Clean your room.

The subjunctive mood refers to wishes or statements contrary to fact.

▶ If I were going to clean my room, I would have done it already.

Avoid abrupt shifts from statements to commands. If a shift is necessary, signal the change to your readers. Alternately, consider more extensive revision.

▶ Next, I will explain how to burn a CD. First, insert the CD into the drive.

The above shift from indicative to imperative is acceptable. The writer eliminates the *I* point of view and prepares the reader to expect technical directions in list format.

SHIFT FROM DIRECT TO INDIRECT DISCOURSE   Direct discourse consists of the actual words of a speaker, with quotation marks around the words. Indirect discourse is a translation or restatement of what the speaker said; no quotation marks are used unless a portion of the original words are included in the restatement. Indirect discourse usually begins with something like "He said that . . ." and is followed by a restatement of the speaker's words.

DIRECT DISCOURSE	President Garcia stated, "I want to see many more low-income students—especially more Hispanic students from the Rio Grande Valley—go to college."
INDIRECT DISCOURSE	President Garcia said that she wanted more low-income students to go to college.

You may not have room to paraphrase the complete meaning, but be especially careful to report the main idea.

3 Errors in Punctuating Sentences

Sentences begin with a capital letter and end with an end punctuation mark, most often a period. Students frequently have difficulty punctuating sentences—using end punctuation when there is no complete sentence (creating a fragment) or punctuating two or more complete sentences as if they were a single sentence (run-on sentence or comma splice).

3a   Fragments

A sentence is a group of words that contains a subject and a finite verb (a verb with tense) and that expresses a complete thought. A sentence fragment is a group of words that is punctuated like a sentence (that is, it begins with a capital letter and ends with end punctuation) but lacks one or more of the elements of a sentence. Although on occasion you might use a fragment intentionally for stylistic effect, it is best to avoid fragments in academic writing.

▶ Although he is a successful businessman. *, he wants to become a teacher*

Be careful not to mistake "although" for "however." "However, he is a successful businessman" *is* a complete sentence.

▶ ~~Whatever~~ you think. *I'll do whatever*

In casual conversation, "Whatever you think" is acceptable. It is not acceptable, however, in academic writing.

**CHECKLIST
4**   **Adding Needed Words to Fragments**

● Supply the missing subject.
  ▶ ~~Went~~ downtown. *She went*

● Supply the missing subject and the correct finite verb.
  ▶ ~~Having~~ known her for twenty years. *I have*

● Attach the fragment to an independent clause.
  ▶ Although she wants to go to college.

  REVISED   Although she wants to go to college, she plans to work for a year before she enrolls.

3b   Comma Splices and Run-On Sentences

A comma splice occurs when independent clauses are joined with a comma rather than with a semicolon or a conjunction (and another clause), or severed with a period. (For more on using semicolons, see pages 57–58.)

▶ The acting was competent*;* the direction was faulty.

Run-on (or fused) sentences are aptly labeled. They run on and on with neither the necessary punctuation to separate them nor the appropriate conjunctions to join them. Sometimes writers create run-on sentences accidentally because they want to link closely related ideas.

▶ I sang softly*, but* it still scared the dog.

Repairing Comma Splices and Run-On Sentences

- Join the independent parts on both sides of the comma splice with a semicolon.

  ▶ I work all day; I exercise in the evening.

- Use subordination to show a clearer relationship between the two independent clauses. Use a conjunction to connect the two independent clauses, thus turning one of them into a dependent clause. Make as many revisions to the sentence as you care to make.

  ▶ Because I sit at a desk all day, I enjoy exercising in the evening.

- End the first sentence with a period. Make the second sentence into a freestanding one. *Note:* Frequently, you must do more than merely insert the punctuation; you may have to revise more extensively if the revised sentences mean more effective paragraph structure.

  ▶ I work all day long. I rush to the gym to exercise in the evening.

4 Effective Word Choice

Adapting your language—your choice of words—to the audience, occasion, and purpose of your papers will help you to communicate your meaning more clearly to readers.

4a Formal and Informal Words

Different words and expressions are appropriate for different occasions. Just as you would not wear cut-offs to a wedding, you would not describe a literary figure as "so cool!" in a paper; to do this would be inappropriately informal.

If you are unsure of the audience and purpose of your writing, maintain a general level of usage. If you know the audience and purpose, then adapt your usage to the context. Keep in mind, however, that words that are either too formal or too casual tend to draw attention to themselves and thus should serve some constructive purpose when used.

If you are writing a letter of application, you might end by using words such as the following:

▶ If you have any questions, please do not hesitate to call.

You would not write a sentence such as this one:

▶ It would be cool if you'd give me a buzz.

Similarly, in a history paper, the following would be inappropriate:

▶ General Lee was a regular kind of guy.

Instead, you might write this:

▶ General Lee was an unassuming leader, one who mixed easily with his troops.

The words "regular kind of guy" are too casual for the purpose of this assignment; the words "unassuming leader" state the same idea in more appropriate words.

Consider the circumstances in which you might use each of the following words or phrases:

FORMAL	INFORMAL
celebration	party
momentous	important
deceased	dead
position	job
wish to	would like to
onerous	difficult
beneficent	generous
misfortune	bad luck

4b   Specific and General Words

Specific words provide precise, sensory, or concrete details. General words convey inexact, intangible, and often abstract concepts. You often want to use general terms in the beginning of a paragraph. Be sure to follow up with sentences that give the reader a more specific notion of what you are talking about.

Some writing tasks require more use of abstractions than others. The degree of specificity required depends on your topic and your focus.

▶ President Bill Clinton's knowledge of domestic issues was superior to his understanding of foreign policy. He was more successful with welfare reform, for example, than with peace in the Middle East.

In this context, "domestic issues" and "foreign policy" are used in a general sense in the first sentence. The writer then elaborates by clarifying specific kinds of issues ("welfare reform" and "peace in the Middle East") referred to by the more general terms in the earlier sentence.

Choosing Precise Words

INSTEAD OF	CONSIDER
a *good* movie	a *suspenseful, terrifying, lighthearted* movie
a *nice* smile	a *winning, angelic, purposeful* smile
someone I know	*a friend, an acquaintance, a colleague*
walked	*paced, strutted, strolled, marched*

4c Figurative Language

Figurative language refers to similes, metaphors, and other rhetorical uses of language. Although effective figurative language can help readers visualize your meaning, ineffective figurative language can ruin the intended effect. In general, state ideas in your own words, and avoid clichés and trite expressions that add nothing distinctive to your meaning. *Note:* A particular danger in using trite expressions is the mixed metaphor, a situation that occurs when a writer unknowingly allows two or more metaphoric images to clash.

▶ If you build your plans on sand, they may collapse.

REVISED   If you don't test the new menu design with users, you can expect complaints.

In the revision, the specific situation is clearly stated in the sentence. In the original, it is not clear what "plans" might "collapse."

▶ Think of your computer screen as a desktop.

The desktop metaphor has helped people understand the concept of keeping files on the top level of the computer screen.

▶ We won by ⌃ ~~leaps and bounds~~ .
　　　　　　　20 points

4d Biased Language

You are expected to use language that avoids bias of any kind. In particular, avoid gender, ethnic, and age bias.

- Use gender-neutral terms: *reporter* rather than *newsman*; *representative* rather than *congressman*.

- Avoid sexist stereotyping.
  - ▸ The ~~wives~~ *spouses* will have an opportunity to tour the city during the conference.

- Use the plural to avoid the awkward use of *he* or *she*.
  - ▸ ~~A~~ *Writers* writer usually revise ~~his or her~~ *their* work several times.

- Avoid age bias.
  - ▸ The ~~kids~~ *young people* can sit at the extra table.
  - ▸ ~~Old~~ *Senior* professors are often more current in their field than their younger colleagues.

- Avoid terms of ethnic bias.
  - ▸ Many ~~Orientals~~ *Asians* live in the outer boroughs.

- Use gender-neutral, nonsexist words.
  - ▸ The ~~stewardess~~ *flight attendant* served the coach passengers a light snack.
  - ▸ The department ~~chairman~~ *head* called a meeting.

- Avoid sexist stereotyping.
  - ▸ If there is a doctor in the house, will he *or she* please step forward?

- Use terms that show respect for people's ethnic backgrounds.
  - ▸ My friend is ~~Oriental~~ *Asian*.

  Or use specific nationality, such as Chinese or Japanese.

  - ▸ Some of the students at the university are Mexican; most of them, however, are Mexican American.

  The term *Mexican* should be used only for individuals who are Mexican nationals.

  - ▸ The black students on many college campuses are not all African Americans. Some blacks are African American; some are African; and others are Islanders from Haiti, Jamaica, and Antigua.

- Use terms that show respect for people's age.

    ▶ She is ~~an old lady~~ *elderly*.

    ▶ ~~Kids~~ *Young people* today are not as willing to read as they were in earlier times.

    ▶ Do you ~~girls~~ *women* want to join us for a golf match?

In the last example, use "women" if you are referring to adults.

5 Usage Glossary

a Use *a* before consonant sounds (*a car, a history, a union*). **an** Use *an* before vowel sounds (*an elk, an X-ray, an herb*).

accept (verb) "to take," "to receive": *I accept the award gladly.* **except** (preposition) "not counting": *Except for the lack of plumbing, the apartment is perfect;* (verb) "to leave out": *Please except that package from the group.*

adapt (verb) "to adjust": *Some people adapt easily to new environments.* **adept** (adjective) "skillful": *She is adept at mastering new tasks.* **adopt** (verb) "to care for as one's own": *He adopts a new image when needed.*

advice (noun) "guidance": *My doctor gave me sound advice.* **advise** (verb) "to recommend," "to inform": *I often advise her on what to wear.*

affect (verb) "to influence": *Technology affects people in different ways.* **effect** (noun) "consequence": *It has both positive and negative effects on job performance;* (verb) "to bring about," "to cause to occur": *Skiing effects a sense of exhilaration.*

aid (noun) "assistance": *Her role is to provide aid to homeless children;* (verb) "to assist": *She aids homeless children.* **aide** (noun) "an assistant": *As an aide, she helps in countless ways.*

allude "to make reference to": *Poets frequently allude to Greek and Roman myths.* **elude** "to avoid capture": *Some poems elude interpretation.*

allusion "indirect reference": *In his footnotes, Eliot explains the allusions in "The Waste Land" to readers.* **illusion** "false appearance": *Her weight loss is an illusion.*

a lot (always two words) "many": *She has a lot of energy.*   alot Incorrect spelling of *a lot*.

all ready "everyone prepared": *The students are all ready to visit the museum.*   already "previously": *Already, the teacher has assigned the first two chapters.*

all right (always two words) "satisfactory," "certainly": *It is all right to admit that you are wrong.*   alright Incorrect spelling of *all right*.

all together "everyone in one place": *When we put our resources all together, we discovered that we had more than we needed to cover our expenses.*   altogether "completely": *You have an altogether different reading list.*

altar (noun) "place of worship": *The altar was decorated with flowers.*   alter (verb) "to change": *The flowers altered the usual appearance of the church.*

among "shared by a group" (usually three or more): *They are among the ten best athletes in the school.*   between "shared by individuals" (usually two): *Tara sat between Julia and Peter.*

amount (noun) "quantity of something that cannot be counted": *The amount of money needed to fund the project is staggering.* (verb) "to equal": *It doesn't amount to much.*   number (noun) "quantity of something that can be counted": *The number of students required for state funding is 750;* (verb) "to include," "to assign a number to": *The chorus numbers twenty.*

anxious "nervous, worried": *I am anxious about my grades.*   eager "characterized by enthusiastic interest": *I am eager to go on vacation.*

any more "no more": *We don't want to buy any more property.*   anymore "any longer": *We don't live here anymore.*

anyone "any person": *Did anyone come?*   any one "any member of a group": *Any one of you would be welcome.*

anyways Nonstandard for *anyway*.

anywheres Nonstandard for *anywhere*.

appraise "to calculate value": *The teacher appraises students' abilities at midterm.*   apprise "to inform": *He apprises them of their strengths and weaknesses.*

as (conjunction) "in the way that": *The computer didn't work as the instructions said it would.*   like (preposition) "similar to": *I would prefer a computer like Anna's.* Do not use *like* in place of *as* or *as if* in formal writing: *They acted as if they were drunk.*

ascent (noun) "rising," "advancement": *The ascent of the rocket into space was swift.* assent (verb) "to agree": *I assent to the compromise;* (noun) "agreement": *After winning the school board's assent, schools began to include Darwinism in the curriculum.*

assistance (noun) "aid": *Work-study students provide assistance in the library.* assistants (plural noun) "helpers": *The librarian always requests additional student assistants.*

bad (adjective) "not good," "sick," "sorry": *This is a bad situation.* badly (adverb) "not well": *We have performed badly.*

bare (adjective) "naked": *I like to walk around with bare feet;* (verb) "to expose": *I bared my soul to the poetry of the moment.* bear (noun) "animal": *The polar bear is an arctic resident;* (verb) "to carry," "to tolerate": *I cannot bear to listen to that music.*

bazaar (noun) "marketplace or fair for the sale of goods": *On our vacation to Mexico, we visited several local bazaars.* bizarre (adjective) "strange": *It was bizarre to run into our neighbors in Mexico.*

because of See *due to/because of.*

beside (preposition) "next to": *We sat beside the president of the company.* besides (preposition) "in addition to," "except": *Besides the members' spouses, we were the only visitors invited;* (adverb) "moreover," "also": *I don't want to go to class; besides, I love the park.*

between See *among/between.*

bring "to move an object toward something": *Bring your roommate to the party.* take "to move an object away from something": *When you exit the train, take your belongings.*

can "to be able to do something": *With practice, you can learn the difference between* can *and* may. may "to ask for or be granted permission": *You may not use* can *in this sentence.*

capital "city in which the seat of government is located": *Santa Fe is the capital of New Mexico;* (noun) "possessions and their value": *If we want more capital, we'll have to raise more money.* capitol "the building that houses the legislature": *In Santa Fe, the capitol is shaped like a Zia sun symbol.*

censer (noun) "incense burner": *The censer gave off a lot of smoke.* censor (verb) "to alter," "to delete": *Many critics would love to censor this artist's work;* (noun) "one who censors": *The censor didn't like my sentence, so he deleted it.* censure (noun) "condemnation"; (verb) "to blame," "to condemn": *The student government censured me for making that statement.*

cite (verb) "to acknowledge": *When you quote someone in a paper, be sure you cite the source.* sight (noun) "ability to see," "something that is seen": *Wearing an eight-foot feathered head-dress, he was a magnificent sight;* (verb) "to glimpse": *In Memphis last week, Elvis was sighted in the supermarket.* site (noun) "location": *The archeological site exposed several layers of human occupation;* (verb) "to place": *I sited the deer tracks in the forest.*

coarse (adjective) "rough": *The texture of the fabric is coarse.* course (noun) "path," "unit of study": *This is a writing course.*

complement (noun) "that which completes": *The baby had the full complement of fingers and toes;* (verb) "to complete": *The printed book complements the online tutorial.* compliment (noun) "expression of admiration": *The author paid Carol a compliment;* (verb) "to flatter": *The author complimented Carol.*

conscience (noun) "sense of right and wrong": *He reads my stories only because he has a guilty conscience.* conscious (adjective) "aware": *He is not conscious of how others react to him.*

continual "repeatedly," "over and over": *Updating our database is a continual process.* continuous "without interruption": *The continuous rivalry between the two of them was harmful.*

could care less Nonstandard for *couldn't care less.*

could of Nonstandard for *could have.*

council (noun) "advisory or legislative body": *The council of elders debated my future.* counsel (noun) "advice": *Her counsel was useful;* (verb) "to give advice": *In the end, they counseled me wisely.*

criteria (plural of criterion) "standard for judgment": *The criteria for choosing the winner were varied.*

data (plural of datum) "facts": *The data are here in this research report.*

defer "to delay," "to yield": *I defer to your judgment.* differ "to disagree," "to be unlike": *I beg to differ with you.*

deference "respect," "consideration": *We turned the music down in deference to those who wanted to sleep.* **difference** "being unlike": *You and I have a difference of opinion.* **diffidence** "shyness": *His diffidence accounts for his lack of a social life.*

desert (noun) "dry, barren place": *The heat of the desert was fierce;* (verb) "to leave": *I will not desert my friends.* **dessert** (noun) "sweet course at the end of a meal": *Dessert is my favorite part of any meal.*

device (noun) "plan," "piece of equipment": *A mouse is a device used to move a pointer in a computer program.* **devise** (verb) "to think up": *Whoever devised the mouse had a great idea.*

different from *Different from* is preferred to *different than: His attitude toward studying is different from mine.* **different than** Use *different than* when a construction using *different from* is wordy: *I am a different person than I was two years ago.*

due to "resulting from": *The bags under my eyes are due to stress.* **because of** "as the result of": *My grade in the class dropped because of this assignment.*

eager See *anxious/eager.*

effect See *affect/effect.*

elude See *allude/elude.*

eminent "prominent," "important": *The professor was eminent in the field.* **immanent** "operating within reality," "inherent": *Knowing which word to use is not an immanent skill—it must be learned.* **imminent** "about to happen": *The test is imminent.*

enthused Use *enthusiastic: The grammarian was enthusiastic when he praised me for never using* enthused.

envelop (verb) "to enclose completely": *The mist will envelop us as soon as we enter the rain forest.* **envelope** (noun) "wrapper, usually for a letter": *Place the invitation in the envelope.*

every one "each individual": *Every one of the athletes was tested for steroid use.* **everyone** "all": *Everyone participated in the talent show.*

except See *accept/except.*

farther "at a greater distance": *Ken's rescue team traveled farther than my team did to help the victims.* **further** "to a greater degree": *Ken explained that further travel was necessary to reach those in need of help.*

few, fewer "a limited number of countable items": *A few of us went to the concert.* little, less "a small quantity of an uncountable item": *It will cost less if you make it yourself.*

formally "not casually": *The rules were formally approved by the city council.* formerly "before": *Formerly, there were no guidelines about sorting household trash.*

good (adjective) not to be used in place of the adverb *well*: *This plan is good.* well (adverb): *The plan will work well.*

hanged "killed by hanging": *The victors hanged their enemies.* hung "suspended": *I hung my clothes out to dry.*

hisself Nonstandard for *himself.*

hopefully "filled with hope": *We moved hopefully toward the future.* Do not use *hopefully* to mean "I hope that," "we hope that," and so forth.

human (noun or adjective) "referring to people": *To be fallible is to be human.* humane (adjective) "compassionate": *The humane treatment of animals is uppermost in Kate's mind.*

illusion See *allusion/illusion.*

immanent See *eminent/immanent/imminent.* imminent See *eminent/immanent/imminent.*

imply "to suggest indirectly": *I don't mean to imply that you are wrong.* infer "to draw a conclusion": *You may have inferred from what I said that I love you.*

incidence "rate of occurrence": *The incidence of heart disease among Americans is high.* incidents "occurrences": *Many incidents during the Revolution led to American patriot losses.*

irregardless Nonstandard for *regardless.*

its (possessive pronoun) "belonging to it": *Its colors were iridescent.* it's contraction for *it is*: *It's a great day.*

kind of/sort of Avoid *kind of* and *sort of* when you mean "somewhat": *The movie was somewhat scary.*

later (adverb) "subsequently": *We'll play with the kitten later.* latter (adjective) "last mentioned": *Of the two stories, I prefer the latter.*

lay (verb + object) "to place something": *He lay the book on the table.* lie (verb + no object) "to assume or be in a reclining position": *He went to his bedroom to lie down.*

lead (verb) "to go before": *If you lead, we will follow*; (noun) "metal," "position at the front": *Anthony Hopkins played the lead.*
led past participle of *lead*: *When you led us yesterday, we followed you.*

less See *few/fewer/little/less.*

lessen (verb) "to decrease": *Your bravery will lessen our fear.*
lesson (noun) "something learned by study or experience": *That is the lesson I learned from you.*

liable "obligated, responsible": *The landlord is liable for the roof repairs.* **likely** "future possibility": *Even if the roof isn't leaking now, it is likely to leak in the future.*

lie See *lay/lie.*

like See *as/like.*

little See *few/fewer/little/less.*

loose (adjective) "not tight": *The bolts on the car door are loose.*
lose (verb) "to misplace," "to not win": *If we invest poorly, we might lose our money.*

many "large number of something countable": *Many of our investments will pay off.* **much** "large number of something uncountable": *Much effort was wasted in this endeavor.*

may See *can/may.*

may be (verb) "might be": *I may be getting better.* **maybe** (adverb) "perhaps": *Maybe we should open a savings account.*

may of Nonstandard for *may have.*

media Plural of *medium: Computers, newspapers, and TV are communications media. Media* has also come to have a singular sense in speech. Formally, use the plural.

might of Nonstandard for *might have.*

much See *many/much.*

must of Nonstandard for *must have.*

nowheres Nonstandard for *nowhere.*

number See *amount/number.*

number of *Number of* should be followed by a plural noun: *a number of options.*

off of *Of* is unnecessary: *Get off the road!*

passed (verb) past tense of *pass: Roaring down the road, he passed me.* past (adjective) "previous": *His past exploits are legendary.*

patience (noun) "ability to wait": *Have some patience.* patient (adjective) "calm": *Be patient;* (noun) "someone receiving medical treatment": *I was his only patient.*

persecute "to harrass": *He felt persecuted by her attentions.* prosecute "to bring to trial": *She was prosecuted for grand larceny.*

personal (adjective) "relating to an individual," "private": *I don't care to share details of my personal life.* personnel (noun) "employees": *The director of personnel takes all new employees to lunch.*

phenomena Plural of *phenomenon,* "observable facts or events": *Like other astronomical phenomena, the eclipse can be easily explained.*

plus Do not use *plus* to join independent clauses; use *moreover* or *in addition to: Your salary in addition to mine will cover our expenses.*

precede "to come before": *She preceded me into the house.* proceed "to go forward," "to continue": *Please proceed carefully into the room.*

prescribe "to order treatment": *The doctor will prescribe a medicine to relieve the pain.* proscribe "to forbid": *Smoking is proscribed here.*

principal (noun) "chief person," "capital sum": *We may earn no interest, but we won't lose the principal;* (adjective) "most important": *The book's principal effect was to change my viewpoint on the economics of ecology.* principle (noun) "rule," "fundamental law": *Tornadoes are based upon physical principles.*

raise (verb + object) "to lift," "to grow": *She raised her arms heavenward;* (noun) "increase in salary." rise (verb + no object) "to get up": *Hot air balloons, however, rise more slowly;* (noun) "ascent," "hilltop": *The rise in temperature was deadly.*

respectfully "with respect": *We behave respectfully around him.* respectively "in the order named": *We saw Kurt, Marian, and Diane, respectively, enter the building.*

right (adjective) "correct": *Roberta was the right woman for the job;* (noun) "something allowed," "location of the right side," "conservative position": *It is their right as Americans.* rite (noun) "ceremony": *For New Yorkers, their first Yankees game is a rite of passage.*

sensual "pleasing to the senses, especially sexual": *Don Juan was addicted to sensual experiences.* sensuous "pleasing to the senses, particularly with regard to the arts": *The poet's use of sensuous detail helped us see, smell, and taste the food.*

set (verb + object) "to place something": *I set the dish on the table.* sit (verb + no object) "to be in or assume a sitting position": *I will sit here and eat my dinner.*

should of Nonstandard for *should have.*

sight See *cite/sight/site.*

site See *cite/sight/site.*

some time (adjective + noun) "span of time": *We have some time before the test begins.* sometime (adverb) "at an unspecified time": *I will probably feel nervous about it sometime soon.* sometimes (adverb) "now and then," "occasionally": *Sometimes I'm funny that way.*

somewheres Nonstandard for *somewhere.*

sort of See *kind of/sort of.*

stationary (adjective) "not moving": *When the wind died, the sailboat was stationary.* stationery (noun) "letter paper": *The captain took out her stationery and wrote a letter to her husband.*

statue "sculpture": *The* Venus de Milo *is a famous statue.* stature "height," "status": *The sculptor had great stature among his peers.* statute "law": *The town has many outdated statutes in its civil code.*

suppose to Incorrect spelling of *supposed to.*

take See *bring/take.*

than (conjunction) used in comparisons: *Learning to sail was easier than learning to windsurf.* then (adverb) "at that time," "besides": *Then I ran the boat aground.*

that Use *that* for essential clauses: *The handbook that we use for English is written by Rodrigues and Tuman.* which Use *which* for nonessential clauses: *The text, which was written by Rodrigues and Tuman, includes suggestions for revising rough drafts.*

their (pronoun) "belonging to them": *Their values are not my values.* there (adverb) "in that place": *"The mouse is over there!" he screamed;* (expletive) used to introduce a sentence or clause: *There are some values I accept.*   **they're** contraction for *they are: They're probably more comfortable than I am.*

theirselves   Nonstandard for *themselves.*

thorough   (adjective) "exhaustive": *His review of my essay was thorough.*   **through**   (preposition) "in and then out": *He did not drive through it with his car;* (adverb) "completely," "finished": *I was soaked through.*

to   (preposition) "toward": *I am going to school.*   **too**   (adverb) "in addition," "excessively": *I am going to the store, too.*   **two**   (noun) "one more than one": *I am going to two places.*

try and   Nonstandard for *try to.*

unique   "one of a kind": *Among actors, Jimmy Stewart is unique.*

use to   Nonstandard for *used to.*

wear   (verb) "to bear or carry on the person," "to cause to degenerate by use": *You can wear what you want.*   **were**   (verb) past tense of *be: You were raised to do the right thing.*   **where** (adverb or conjunction) "in that place": *You can go where you want.*

weather   (noun) "atmosphere": *The weather outside is frightful.*   **whether**   (conjunction) "if": *I don't know whether it will ever be delightful.*

well   See *good/well.*

which   See *that/which.*

which/who   Do not use *which* to refer to people; use *who: She is the person who helped me the most.*

who   Use *who* for subjects and subject complements: *I will check to see who is at the door.*   **whom**   Use *whom* for objects: *I am the person whom she helped.*

who's   Contraction of *who is: Who's this sweating at the table?*   **whose**   (pronoun) possessive form of *who: He's the person whose tongue is burning from the chili peppers.*

would of   Nonstandard for *would have.*

your   (pronoun) "belonging to you": *Your cleverness amazes me.*   **you're**   Contraction for *you are: You're a clever person.*

Grammar

6 Verbs

Verbs express action or show a state of existence (*be* verbs) by linking the subject to the rest of the sentence. Sentences must have at least one verb, but they can have several. Verbs indicate the tense or time an action or state of existence occurred, is occurring, or will occur.

▶ The top salesperson *sold* more than fifty cars last month. [action in the past]

▶ The book *is available* in the bookstore at the beginning of the term. [state of being in the present]

Verbs often use auxiliary or helping words such as *had, can, might, will,* or *would* to form different tenses.

▶ The book *will be* available in June. [future]

▶ The ship *might have been* seaworthy. [conditional]

6a Subject-Verb Agreement

The subject and verb in a sentence or clause must agree or match. If the subject is singular, the verb must be singular; if the subject is plural, the verb must be plural. If the subject is in the first person (*I, we*), the verb must be in the first person (*I am, we are*). The same rule holds true for subjects in the second person or third person (*you are; he/she/it is, they are*).

	SINGULAR	PLURAL
FIRST PERSON	I sing	we sing
SECOND PERSON	you sing	you sing
THIRD PERSON	he/she/it sings	they sing

INTERVENING WORDS Sometimes a word or phrase comes between the subject and the verb. Ignore that word or phrase when locating the subject and verb, making sure that the verb agrees with the subject.

- ▶ My *brother*, along with our friends, *is* looking forward to this weekend.
- ▶ One of my friends _{is} ~~are~~ graduating.

Hint: To test subject-verb agreement, mentally recite the sentence *without* the intervening words. That is, replace the complete subject "one of my friends is graduating" with "one is graduating."

COMPOUND SUBJECTS JOINED BY *AND* When the parts of a subject are joined by *and*, the verb is usually plural.

- ▶ Captain Janeway and three other officers *were* honored.
- ▶ The coach and the quarterback *understand* what teamwork means.

The exception occurs when the subject is a single item, like a food dish (for example, *strawberries and cream*), formed by joining together two items.

- ▶ Red beans and rice *is* a popular dish in Louisiana.

Hint: To make subject-and-verb agreement easier, try substituting a pronoun for the compound subject. For instance, in the football example, above, substituting "they" for the compound subject "the coach and the quarterback" results in "they understand."

COMPOUND SUBJECT JOINED BY *OR* OR *NOR* When parts of a subject are joined by *or* or *nor*, the verb agrees with the closer noun.

- ▶ Neither my mother nor my other relatives _{are} ~~is~~ happy with the decision.
- ▶ Either the administrators or the union _{is} ~~are~~ to blame.

INDEFINITE PRONOUNS AS SUBJECTS Indefinite pronouns refer to nonspecific individuals (*anybody, anyone, each, either, everybody, everyone, everything, neither, none, no one, somebody, someone, something*) and, hence, seem to be plural. However, most are singular.

- ▶ Everyone *likes* English.
- ▶ None of us *has* classes today.

Note: There is a tendency to use the plural possessive-pronoun form *their* to refer to indefinite pronouns since it conveniently refers to both males and females. Most teachers and editors, however, still expect the standard rule for agreement to be followed—hence, the need for *his or her*, as in "Everyone should turn in his or her final draft." Of course, one could be more concise and say, "Students should turn in their final drafts."

Some indefinite pronouns are always plural (*few, many*).

▶ Many *are called*, but few *are chosen*.

Some indefinite pronouns (*all, any, some*) are either singular or plural, depending on the noun or pronoun to which they refer.

▶ All of the students [plural] *like* English.

▶ All of the water [singular] *is* gone.

COLLECTIVE NOUNS AS SUBJECTS   Most collective nouns (nouns that refer to a group) are considered singular.

▶ The *class has selected* her president.

▶ The *group wants* to remain seated.

Numerical collective nouns are either singular or plural, depending on whether the focus of the sentence is on the group or on the individual members of the group.

▶ A *majority* of team members *have* injuries.

▶ A *majority* of team members *has* selected Barbara as captain.

In the first sentence, the focus is on the many team members who have injuries. In the second, the team members in the majority are considered as a unit.

REVERSED SUBJECTS AND VERBS   The verb must agree with its grammatical subject even when the subject appears after the verb. When the subject of a sentence is placed after the verb, identifying the subject can be tricky. Remember that expressions such as *there is* and *there are* (expletives) do not contain the subject. (See section 1d, page 6, for a discussion of expletives.)

▶ There are thirty days in April.

▶ Reckless driving and speeding was the explanation for the traffic ticket.

SENTENCES WITH SUBJECT COMPLEMENTS A subject complement is a word or group of words that substitutes for the subject. A subject complement can easily be mistaken for the subject since it renames the subject.

▶ The *main requirement* of the job *is* a commitment to music and a demonstration of that commitment through station programming.

The verb "is" agrees with the singular subject "main requirement," not with the subject complement "commitment to music and a demonstration of that commitment through station programming."

VERBS AFTER *THAT, WHICH, AND WHO* The relative pronouns *that, which*, and *who* can be either singular or plural, depending on their antecedents—the word or words to which they refer.

▶ Students are one of the groups [plural] who are suffering from reductions in federal programs.

▶ A student [singular] who is ill should go to the health center.

It is not always immediately obvious if the antecedent is singular or plural. In the following example, "one of the" creates a plural meaning.

▶ The quality of the olive oil is *one of the* things [plural] that make some Italian dishes better than others.

Hint: To figure out what the verb should be, isolate the one word that can substitute for the subject—in this case "things"—and mentally state the simplified sentence that results: "Things make dishes better."

SINGULAR NOUNS ENDING IN *-S* Words that end in *-s* such as *academics, statistics, mathematics*, and *physics* are frequently singular.

▶ At some schools, *athletics is* stressed more than studying.

▶ *Statistics is* feared by many a graduate student.

A title containing plural nouns is singular.

▶ *Hard Times* is a beloved Dickens novel.

Use the plural form when suggesting separate activities or characteristics.

▶ The statistics of war are shocking.

6b Irregular Verbs

Verbs change form to show changes in tense or time. Regular verbs form their past tense and past participle by adding -d (for example, *care, cared*), -ed (for example, *walk, walked*), or -t (for example, *burn, burnt*). Irregular verbs form their past tense and past participle in many different ways. Irregular verb forms must be memorized. The following table gives the past tense and past participle of some common irregular verbs.

Common Irregular Verbs

PRESENT TENSE	PAST TENSE	PAST PARTICIPLE
arise	arose	arisen
awake	awoke, awaked	awaked, awoke
be	was, were	been
beat	beat	beaten, beat
become	became	become
begin	began	begun
bend	bent	bent
bite	bit	bitten, bit
blow	blew	blown
break	broke	broken
bring	brought	brought
build	built	built
burst	burst	burst
buy	bought	bought
catch	caught	caught
choose	chose	chosen
cling	clung	clung
come	came	come
cost	cost	cost
deal	dealt	dealt
dig	dug	dug
dive	dived, dove	dived
do	did	done
drag	dragged	dragged
draw	drew	drawn
dream	dreamed, dreamt	dreamed, dreamt
drink	drank	drunk

PRESENT TENSE	PAST TENSE	PAST PARTICIPLE
drive	drove	driven
eat	ate	eaten
fall	fell	fallen
feel	felt	felt
fight	fought	fought
find	found	found
fly	flew	flown
forget	forgot	forgotten, forgot
freeze	froze	frozen
get	got	gotten, got
give	gave	given
go	went	gone
grow	grew	grown
hang (suspend)	hung	hung
hang (execute)	hanged	hanged
have	had	had
hear	heard	heard
hide	hid	hidden
hold	held	held
hurt	hurt	hurt
keep	kept	kept
know	knew	known
lay (put)	laid	laid
lead	led	led
lend	lent	lent
let (allow)	let	let
lie (recline)	lay	lain
lose	lost	lost
make	made	made
prove	proved	proved, proven
read	read	read
ride	road	ridden
ring	rang	rung
rise	rose	risen
run	ran	run
say	said	said
see	saw	seen
send	sent	sent
set (put)	set	set
shake	shook	shaken
shine	shone	shone
shoot	shot	shot

PRESENT TENSE	PAST TENSE	PAST PARTICIPLE
shrink	shrank	shrunk, shrunken
sing	sang	sung
sink	sank	sunk
sit (be seated)	sat	sat
slay	slew	slain
sleep	slept	slept
speak	spoke	spoken
spin	spun	spun
spring	sprang	sprung
stand	stood	stood
steal	stole	stolen
sting	stung	stung
strike	struck	struck, stricken
swear	swore	sworn
swim	swam	swum
swing	swung	swung
take	took	taken
teach	taught	taught
throw	threw	thrown
wake	woke, waked	waked, woken
wear	wore	worn
wring	wrung	wrung
write	wrote	written

7 Pronoun Agreement

Pronouns —*she, he, it, them*, and so forth—are words that substitute for nouns. Pronouns must agree with their antecedents —the word or words to which they refer—and with the verb in the sentence by agreeing in number and case.

7a Pronoun-Antecedent Agreement

Use singular pronouns to refer to singular nouns and plural pronouns to refer to plural nouns.

▶ *Steve* argued for *his* position, but his *friends* preferred *their* own plans.

▶ *Everyone* voted for *his or her* favorite candidate.

"Everyone" is singular; therefore, "his" or "her" (singular pronouns) is used.

	SINGULAR		
Checking Personal and Possessive Pronouns		**CHECKLIST 8**	

		SINGULAR		
SECOND PERSON	I	me	my	mine
SECOND PERSON	you	you	your	yours
THIRD PERSON	he/she/it	him/her/it	his/her/its	his/her/its
		PLURAL		
FIRST PERSON	we	us	our	ours
SECOND PERSON	you	you	your	yours
THIRD PERSON	they	them	their	theirs

7b With the Conjunctions *and*, *or*, and *nor*

Use a plural pronoun to refer to two nouns or pronouns joined by *and*.

▶ *The instructor and the student* agreed that *they* should meet.

▶ *He and I* asked if *we* could collaborate on the next assignment.

Use a singular pronoun to refer to two singular nouns joined by *or* or *nor*.

▶ Either *Michael or Jason* can take *his* turn first.

If you have one singular and one plural noun joined by *or* or *nor*, place the plural noun in the second position and use a plural pronoun.

▶ Neither *Maggie nor her three sisters* have received *their* checks.

7c Indefinite Pronoun Antecedents

Indefinite pronouns that are singular should be referred to by singular pronouns.

▶ *Each* of the colleges has *its* own admissions policy.

Some indefinite pronouns are plural (*both*, *few*, *many*) and require plural pronouns.

▶ A *few* of the players have yet to pass *their* physicals.

Some indefinite pronouns may be either singular or plural (*all*, *any*, *some*). A pronoun referring to one of these indefinite pronouns is singular if the indefinite pronoun referred to stresses the action of an entire group as a whole; it is plural if it refers to the various situations of members of the group.

▶ *Some* of the *play* was entertaining.

▶ *Some* of the *costumes* are grotesque.

7d With Collective Nouns

Treat collective nouns (*class*, *team*, *audience*, *committee*, and so forth) as singular if you are stressing the group's acting as a unit; treat them as plural if you are stressing the actions of the group's individual members.

▶ The *class* will take *its* final exam on Monday.

▶ The *class* immediately began to register *their* protests.

Do not treat the same noun as both singular and plural in the same sentence.

▶ The class was stunned but then registered their protests.

REVISED The students in the class were stunned but then registered their protests.

7e Gender-Inclusive Pronouns

When referring to a singular noun that may be either male or female, use *his or her*, not *his* alone. If you wish to avoid using *his or her* (which, when overused, can sound awkward), switch to the plural.

▶ *A doctor's* responsibility is to *his or her* patients.

REVISED *Doctors* are responsible for *their* patients.

▶ A *parent* should take good care of *his* children.

REVISED *Parents* should take good care of *their* children.

8 Pronoun Case

Case refers to the way a pronoun functions in a sentence—as a subject (nominative case), as an object (objective case), or to show possession (possessive case). Pronouns must be used in the proper case form.

▶ It is *she* who must be obeyed.

In this sentence, "she" functions as a subject and must be in the nominative case.

▶ We elected *her* president.

In this sentence, "her" is the object and thus is in the objective case.

▶ The president wanted to know if *his* changes to the agenda had been added.

In this sentence, "his" shows possession.

Checking Case Forms of Pronouns
CHECKLIST 9

NOMINATIVE CASE	OBJECTIVE CASE	POSSESSIVE CASE
I	me	my
we	us	our
you	you	your
he/she/it	him/her/it	his/her/its
they	them	their

8a   With Appositives

Appositives mean the same thing as the word to which they refer.

▶ Dr. Jefferson, *my physics professor*, just retired.

Appositives and the nouns to which they refer (their antecedents) should be in the same case.

▶ The handout was for the only two sophomores in the class, Ramon and *me*.

Hint: When you read the sentence to yourself, test it with only a pronoun in the appositive position. Listen to the sound of your sentence. You would not say: "The handout was for I." You would say: "The handout was for me."

Use the subjective case when the pronoun acts as a subject.

▶ Loyal friends, Jennifer and *I* decided to stay in spite of the rain.

Hint: "I decided to stay."

Use the objective case when the pronoun acts as an object.

▶ The lawyer asked the witnesses, Addy and *me*, to testify.

Hint: "The lawyer asked me to testify."

(See Checklist 8, page 37, for a review of how to form plural pronouns in different cases.)

8b With Incomplete Comparisons

When using pronouns to compare two nouns, avoid using in complete sentence structures or elliptical constructions. Such sentences omit words and require careful use of pronouns. Be sure sentences convey the meaning that you intend them to convey.

▶ James likes sailing more than *I*.

This sentence means that James likes sailing more than I like sailing. The writer has omitted the words "like sailing" from the end of the sentence.

▶ James likes sailing more than *me*.

This sentence means that James likes sailing more than he likes me. The writer has used "more than me" instead of "more than he likes me."

8c With Subjects of Infinitives

Subjects of infinitives should be in the objective case.

▶ We wanted *him* to see the photographs.

"Him" is the subject of the infinitive phrase "him to see the photographs." *Hint:* First identify the subject and the verb: "We wanted." Next identify the object by asking, Who or what did we want? The answer: "him to see the photographs." The entire phrase is the object of the sentence. The object happens to include its own subject—"him."

8d Before Gerunds

Pronouns before gerunds (-*ing* words used as nouns) must be in the possessive case.

▶ *His* walking away showed good judgment.

The "walking away" is owned by him. To show ownership, use the possessive case.

Sometimes an *-ing* word preceded by a pronoun is not a gerund phrase, but a participial phrase. Consider the following sentence:

▶ I saw *him* walking away.

In this sentence, the object is "him," which is modified by "walking away," a participial phrase.

8e Pronoun Reference

Pronoun reference in a sentence must be clear. Readers should have no trouble figuring out to whom or to what a pronoun refers. Revise sentences with ambiguous references, even if you have to repeat a reference rather than use the pronoun.

AMBIGUOUS   Americans admire movie stars because *they* are wealthy and attractive.

REVISED   Americans admire movie stars because *movie stars* are wealthy and attractive.

In the first sentence, "they" can refer to either "Americans" or "movie stars."

AMBIGUOUS   The new prison has updated facilities, but *they* still treat inmates harshly.

REVISED   The new prison has updated facilities, but *the prison officials* still treat inmates harshly.

Grammatically, "they" refers to "facilities" in the first sentence. Actually, "they" refers to "the prison officials," which is implied but not mentioned in that sentence.

PRONOUN REFERENCE WITH RELATIVE PRONOUNS   *That, which, who, whoever, whom, whomever,* and *whose* are relative pronouns, pronouns that relate or connect parts of sentences. Use *who* or *whom* to refer to people; use *that* to refer to objects. Informally, *that* is sometimes used to refer to a class of people.

▶ I surprised *whoever* was there.

"Whoever" is the subject of the clause "was there."

▶ She was the only one in the class *who* had been to Mexico.

▶ The place *that* she wanted to see was Mexico.

Note: Use *who* or *whoever* in the subject position of a sentence; use *whom* or *whomever* if the pronoun functions as an object. When you want to refer to one or more things rather than to people, use *which* or *that.*

▶ The antiques *that* we bought in Philadelphia are from the eighteenth century.

The clause "that we bought in Philadelphia" is an essential clause (see the next section) and should not be set off with commas.

▶ Our antiques, *which* are primarily in the upstairs rooms, do not match the style of our contemporary home.

The clause "which are primarily in the upstairs rooms" is a nonessential clause (see the next section) and must be set off with commas.

PRONOUN REFERENCE WITH *THAT* AND *WHICH* IN ESSENTIAL AND NONESSENTIAL CLAUSES   Use *that* to introduce expressions that are essential to the meaning of a sentence. Use *which* to introduce nonessential expressions. Set off nonessential clauses with commas. (See section 12d, pages 54–55.)

▶ The game *that* I remember best was the only one we lost.

In this sentence, the writer wants to make a point that of all the games he or she remembers, there is one that stands out.

▶ The game, *which* I remember well, was the only one we lost.

In this sentence, the *which* expression is presented as an afterthought, something not essential to the meaning of the sentence. The commas set the idea aside, much as parentheses do.

Avoid using *that* or *which* to refer to a general state of affairs implied, but not necessarily specified, in your writing.

▶ I was concerned ~~that~~ because you had not called.

▶ ~~That~~ This sentence needs to be revised.

9   Adjectives and Adverbs

9a   Adjectives

Adjectives modify nouns and pronouns. They can be words, phrases, or clauses.

▶ We had *rainy* weather.

▶ The *stone* walls have been standing for *more than two hundred* years.

The italicized words and phrases in the above sentences are adjectives.

Adjectives usually follow verb forms of *be, seem, appear,* and *become*; sensory words such as *taste, touch,* and *feel*; and a few other verbs, including *grow, prove, get, keep, remain,* and *turn.*

▶ I am *happy.*

▶ It tastes *good.*

▶ She has been proved *wrong.*

9b Adverbs

Adverbs modify verbs, adjectives, and other adverbs. Adverbs can be a single word, a phrase, or a clause. Adverbs are often formed by adding *-ly* to adjectives.

▶ It rained *softly.*

▶ It rained *in the evening.*

▶ *When it rained*, we went inside.

Sometimes the same word can function as either an adverb or an adjective, depending on its meaning in a sentence.

▶ Kristen is feeling *well.*

"Well" (meaning "healthy") is an adjective, modifying the subject.

▶ She did *well* on the test.

"Well" is an adverb, modifying the verb.

▶ Drive *slowly* in a school zone.

"Slowly" is an adverb, modifying the verb "drive."

▶ The car functions best at *slow* speeds.

"Slow" is an adjective, modifying the noun "speeds."

9c Comparatives and Superlatives

Adverbs and adjectives have three forms: the positive form (which is the adverb or adjective itself), the comparative form (which compares two things), and the superlative form (which compares three or more things). In general, form the comparative or the superlative by adding -*er* and -*est* to the base.

▶ I ride *faster* than Jordan.

▶ Jeremy rides the *fastest*.

With words ending in -*ly*, however, the comparative and superlative are formed by adding the words *more* and *most* (or *less* and *least*) before the adverb.

▶ She rides *more quickly*.

POSITIVE	COMPARATIVE	SUPERLATIVE
fast	faster	fastest
quickly	more quickly	most quickly

With longer adjectives, the comparative and superlative are also formed by adding *more* and *most* (or *less* and *least*) before the adjective.

▶ the *most beautiful* view.

POSITIVE	COMPARATIVE	SUPERLATIVE
pretty	prettier	prettiest
beautiful	more beautiful	most beautiful

10 Grammar Tips for Multilingual Writers

Some features of English pose difficulties for students who are multilingual. This section reviews some problem areas for those who've learned English as a second language.

10a Articles (*a, an, the*)

Articles—*a, an, the*—indicate that the word following them is a noun. Learn how to use *a, an,* and *the* correctly with both countable and uncountable nouns. Also learn when no article is needed.

WHEN TO USE *A* OR *AN*

1. Use *a* or *an* when a singular, countable noun is not known to the reader or listener.

   ▶ *A* cat is on the doorstep.

"A cat" is correct if you do not know the animal. "Cat" is a "countable" noun. You can count the number of cats in a kennel.

▶ *A* ticket costs fifty dollars.

"A ticket" is correct because you have not yet purchased the specific ticket you will use. "Ticket" is a countable noun. You can count the number of tickets available for sale.

2. Use *a* before countable nouns that begin with a consonant.

   ▶ *a* cat, *a* radio, *a* college campus

3. Use *an* before countable nouns that begin with a vowel and before consonants that begin with a silent *h*.

   ▶ *an* elephant, *an* hour

WHEN TO USE *THE*

1. Use *the* when the noun (singular or plural) is already familiar to the reader or listener.

   ▶ *The* cat is on *the* couch again.

   ▶ *The* ticket for tonight's show is on *the* table.

2. Use *the* with singular, uncountable nouns.

   ▶ *The* milk is in the refrigerator.

   ▶ *The* food is on the table.

WHEN NOT TO USE AN ARTICLE

1. Do not use an article with singular proper nouns that refer to a specific place.

   ▶ I visited Atlanta, Georgia, last summer.

   Note: Use *the* with some geographical areas—for example, *the South, the Northeast, the United States.*

2. Do not use an article when you want to indicate a general category.

   Car
   ▶ ~~The car~~ emissions can pollute the environment.
      ^

   Note: The original sentence indicates that a specific type of car emission can pollute the environment.

10b Adjectives and Adverbs

PLACEMENT OF ADJECTIVES AND ADVERBS IN SENTENCES
Adjectives are placed differently in English than in some other languages. In English, the standard order is adverb-adjective-noun, as in *especially healthy students*.

Adverbs can appear in the following positions:

- At the beginning of a sentence

  ▶ *Cautiously*, she moved up the steps.

- At the end of a sentence

  ▶ She moved up the steps *cautiously*.

- Before the main verb

  ▶ She *cautiously* moved up the steps.

- After the main verb

  ▶ She moved *cautiously* up the steps.

- Before, between, and after helping and main verbs

  ▶ *Cautiously*, she would move up the steps.

  ▶ She would move *cautiously* up the steps.

  ▶ She would *cautiously* move up the steps.

  Note: Not all adverbs can be placed after helping verbs.

  ▶ The student can find usually ᶠⁱⁿᵈ errors in his sentences.
      ∧

ADJECTIVES USED WITH COUNT AND NONCOUNT NOUNS
Notice whether the noun you are using is a "count" noun (such as *bananas, steak, peas*) or a "noncount" noun (such as *fruit, meat, vegetables*). Then determine which adjective is appropriate to use with the noun in question.

Many/much   Use *many* with count nouns; use *much* with noncount nouns.

- ▶ There are *many bananas* on the table. [You can count bananas.]

- ▶ There is too *much fruit* on the table. [You can't count fruit; it's a general category.]

- ▶ There are *many people* in the class. [You can count the people.]

- ▶ There is *much human error* involved. [You can't count human error; it's a quality.]

▶ There are *many days* when we have good weather in April. [Days can be counted.]

▶ There is not *much good weather* in January. [You can't count weather; it's a general concept.]

A few/a little Use *a few* with count nouns; use *a little* with non-count nouns.

▶ You can give me *a few ideas*. [You can count ideas.]

▶ Can you give me *a little help*. [You can't count help; it's a concept.]

Number/amount Use *number* with count nouns; use *amount* with noncount nouns.

▶ You have a large *number of students* at your university.

▶ It takes a large *amount of money* to go to college.

10c Verbs

Verb forms in English can cause problems for students for whom English is a second language. Below are the major areas to focus on if you have problems with verbs.

HELPING VERBS Helping or auxiliary verbs combine with verb forms to form different tenses and include *am, are, be, been, being, can, could, did, do, does, had, has, have, is, may, might, must, shall, should, was, were, will,* and *would.*

A helping verb must come before the base form or the infinitive form of the verb. For more on verb tense, see below.

▶ She *has* helped me for many years.

"Has" comes before the base form of the verb *help.*

▶ They *must* learn how to study.

"Must" comes before the main verb "learn."

▶ I *have* to go home.

"Have" comes before the infinitive "to go."

Do is used as a helping verb to form questions and negative statements.

▶ *Did* you enjoy your trip to Mexico?

▶ My sister *did not* travel with me to Mexico.

After *do* and some helping verbs (such as *can, could, may,* or *might*), a verb is often used alone, without sentence modifiers following it. Note that in the following examples there is no *-s* added to the verbs "care" or "happen."

► She does *care*.

► It could *happen*.

CHANGES IN VERB TENSE   Rather than trying to memorize rules for using different tenses, listen to and practice correct combinations. Below is a table for reference.

PRESENT	PAST	FUTURE
SIMPLE:		
I study	I studied	I will study
PROGRESSIVE *(refers to an action in progress or unfinished):*		
I am studying	I was studying	I will be studying
PERFECT *(refers to an action that began in the past but continues in the present):*		
I have studied	I had studied	I will have studied
PERFECT PROGRESSIVE *(refers to an action that began in the past, continues in the present, and may continue in the future):*		
I have been studying	I had been studying	I will have been studying

10d Idiomatic Expressions

IDIOMATIC PHRASES   All languages have expressions that are understandable to native speakers but almost untranslatable to others. These expressions are referred to as idioms or idiomatic phrases. If you are a bilingual student, try to listen for these phrases and memorize them. Gradually, you will use them in the proper situations, just as people who have spoken English for their entire lives do. Often these idioms are metaphors—imaginative uses of language—such as *keep your eye on the ball* (meaning "be observant") or *cut the mustard* (meaning "do the job"). Other times they are merely phrases, such as *think it over, get going, on the contrary,* and *above all*.

Many verbs in English are commonly used with a preposition and are, in effect, a special kind of idiom. Two-word combinations, such as *graduate from, insist on, back off, turn on,* and *turn off* are not easy for speakers for whom English is not their first language. The best advice is to keep a list of two-word verbs and their meanings and to memorize them.

10e Complete Sentences

In some languages, one word can serve as both subject and predicate. In English, only imperative sentences can omit the subject (the subject, "you," is understood). Other sentences require both a subject and a verb.

▶ *Look* at the stop sign.

▶ ~~Bought~~ a ticket. *(I bought)*

▶ The animals *(were)* outside in the cold.

When the subject follows the verb, an expletive (*there is, there are, it is,* and so forth) is usually required.

▶ *It is* usually cold in Minnesota.

Introductory words can sometimes confuse nonnative speakers into omitting expletives.

▶ Although we were comfortable, *(it)* was always cold in Minnesota.

Do not omit the verb in sentences like

▶ He *(is)* a very good cook.

Punctuation

11 End Punctuation

Every sentence must end with either a period, a question mark, or an exclamation point.

11a The Period [.]

Use a period at the end of statements, mild commands, or indirect questions.

▶ The banks are closed today.

▶ Please shut down your computer at the end of the day.

▶ I wonder what happened to him.

11b The Question Mark [?]

Use a question mark at the end of direct questions and within parentheses and dashes to indicate uncertainty within a sentence.

▶ What happened to him?

▶ It was early (before 6 A.M.?).

11c The Exclamation Point [!]

Use an exclamation point at the end of assertions of surprise or other strong emotions.

▶ "He's alive!" Dr. Frankenstein screamed.

▶ Don't run on the sidewalk! It's slippery.

Do not overuse exclamation points. Reserve them for special effects, such as in the above examples, and remember that one exclamation point works better than a string of three or four to signal heightened feeling.

12 The Comma [,]

Writers use commas according to a handful of basic rules involving signaling pauses within sentences and clarifying structure.

12a In Compound Sentences

Unless the sentences are short, use a comma between two independent clauses joined by a coordinating conjunction (*and, but, for, nor, or, so, yet*) to signal the end of one clause and the beginning of the next.

▶ The judge listened attentively, but many of the jurors had trouble following the testimony.

The comma can be omitted in short, parallel sentences.

▶ The judge listened attentively but many of the jurors did not.

A comma is *not* used when a coordinating conjunction links the parts of a compound verb.

▶ The judge listened attentively but ruled against the motion.

12b After Most Introductory Material

Use a comma after introductory material to signal to the reader that the main part of the sentence is beginning. The comma may be omitted if the introductory material is brief and flows directly into the main clause.

▶ Nevertheless, we decided to continue.

▶ Although most film critics disliked the movie, it enjoyed great success at the box office.

▶ In some cities the movie enjoyed great success at the box office.

12c Between Items in a Series

A comma is used to separate each item in a series. Usually, *and* or *or* is used before the last item.

▶ I am studying statistics, astronomy, and physics.

▶ Next term, I plan to take algebra, chemistry, or geology.

Each item in a series can itself consist of many words.

▶ The mayor was delighted that the city council approved the new parking garage, defeated changes in the zoning ordinance, and delayed consideration of increases in sewerage rates.

When each item in a series includes commas, a semicolon is used to separate the items.

▶ The mayor was delighted that the city council approved the new parking garage, the one to be built near city hall; defeated changes in the zoning ordinance, changes that would have helped save many old neighborhoods; and delayed consideration of increases in sewerage rates.

A series may consist of only two words, as in the case of coordinate (or reversible) adjectives before a noun.

▶ *Halloween* is a suspenseful, terrifying movie.

or

▶ *Halloween* is a terrifying, suspenseful movie.

Do not use a comma with adjectives whose order in a sequence is not reversible.

▶ We saw a new Australian movie.

The adjectives "new" and "Australian" are not reversible. You would not say "an Australian new movie."

12d　With Nonessential Words and Phrases

Use commas around words that are nonessential and could be omitted without loss of meaning. Nonessential material may be informative or interesting, but it is always extra information, not information that narrows and, thus, helps to identify the subject under consideration.

Remember two things when using commas to distinguish between essential and nonessential material: (1) always use a pair of commas to separate nonessential material, one on each side of the material, and (2) when in doubt about whether something is nonessential or not, leave the commas out. (See also section 8e, page 41.)

▶ Graduates *who are adept at using computers* have an advantage in the job market.

The example above assumes that these graduates have an advantage over those graduates who are not adept at using computers.

▶ Graduates, *who are adept at using computers*, have an advantage in the job market.

That is, graduates generally have this particular advantage over nongraduates. The information about their computer skills is offered here as something extra; the sentence can be read without the words between the commas.

12e   Other Comma Rules

Some comma rules do not fit into categories. Think of these rules as ones that apply only in certain circumstances.

1. Use commas to prevent misreading.

   ▶ Soon after, Stephen Bill left the room.

2. Use commas to indicate omitted words.

   ▶ Tim donated $50; Robert, $100.

3. Use commas to set off the year when the month and day are also given.

   ▶ The hearing was set for May 12, 2005, but it actually began in July.

4. Use commas to set off the name of a state, county, or country that follows the name of a city.

   ▶ Our Fresno, California, location has three stores to serve you.

5. Use commas with contrasting expressions (*but, not, rather than*) that emphasize a sense of contrast.

   ▶ The managers promoted Jonah, rather than Mike.

12f   Comma Problems

1. Do not be fooled by the pause and punctuate the subject of a sentence as an introductory phrase.

   ▶ To create a successful Web site, requires considerable planning.

2. Do not use a comma between compound verbs (verbs joined by *or* or *and*).

▶ We studied for the test, and developed our confidence.

In this sentence, "studied" and "developed" are compound verbs and are, therefore, not separated by a comma.

3. Do not use commas inconsistently.

▶ Since it is a beautiful day, I think I'll go for a walk.

▶ Because I have little time, I rarely exercise during the work week.

If you use a comma after an introductory phrase, do so consistently throughout your paper.

4. Although commas should be used to separate the nonessential material from the rest of the sentence, do not use a comma to separate two complete sentences. Doing so creates a comma splice. (See section 3b, page 14.)

▶ Talk is cheap ~~,~~ . Action ~~action~~ is what counts.

▶ You shouldn't be concerned about grammar as you draft ~~,~~ . You ~~you~~ should focus on content and organization.

5. Do not forget the second comma in nonessential phrases. Think of these two commas as if they were parentheses.

▶ Computer viruses, often compared to physical diseases, are common on our campus.

CHECKLIST 10 A Quick Review of Comma Rules

USE A COMMA
- between two independent clauses joined by one of the seven coordinating conjunctions: *and, but, for, nor, or, so, yet.*
- after most introductory material.
- between coordinate items in a series.
- before and after nonessential words and phrases.
- as called for according to convention or to prevent misreading.

13 The Semicolon [;] and Colon [:]

13a The Semicolon [;]

In addition to using the semicolon between series items with internal commas (see section 12c, pages 53–54), the semicolon can be used to join closely connected independent clauses that are not otherwise connected by a coordinating conjunction. The basic rule in using semicolons is to be sure that you have complete sentences (independent clauses) on both sides of the semicolon.

▶ The rain never ceased; it continued throughout the night and into the next week.

▶ Time went quickly; before she knew it, she was too old to find a good job.

The semicolon strengthens the connection between the two ideas that, if joined by a period, might be read as two separate, less related sentences. Be careful, however, not to use a comma, which in such cases would create a comma splice. (See section 3b, page 14.)

Hence, however, indeed, moreover, still, therefore, thus, and similar terms are adverbs (sometimes called conjunctive adverbs) that belong entirely to the second sentence. Therefore, they cannot be used like a coordinating conjunction to join two sentences. When used after a semicolon, they are followed by a comma. When used as interrupters within independent clauses, they are set off with commas.

▶ Homer found it difficult to beg forgiveness; however, Marge eventually forgave him.

▶ Homer found it difficult to beg forgiveness; Marge, however, eventually forgave him.

13b Semicolon Problems

Do not use a semicolon in sentences that do not contain two independent clauses. Use a comma instead.

▶ The interview went well; better than I expected.

The phrase "better than I expected" is not an independent clause. It is a phrase that modifies the entire sentence and that can be separated from the sentence with a comma.

▶ As time passed; I knew I was going to like her.

The first part of the above sentence is an introductory clause (acting as an adverb) and must be connected to the independent clause with a comma.

13c   The Colon [:]

Within a sentence, a colon announces a list, a question, or a complete sentence that follows it.

1. Use a colon after an independent clause to introduce a list, a direct quotation, or an explanation.

   ▶ These are the key factors to consider when purchasing software: price, performance, and support.

   ▶ Confucius says: "It is easy to be rich and not haughty; it is difficult to be poor and not grumble."

   ▶ When the time is right, you'll know it: You'll be ready to get married, and you'll want to do it without delay.

   It is appropriate to capitalize the first word of a complete sentence following a colon.

2. Use a colon after salutations in formal business letters.

   ▶ Dear Dr. Bartholomew:

   ▶ Dear Admissions Committee:

   Instead of saying "Dear Sir or Madam," use a noun to substitute for the person to whom you are addressing the letter.

3. Use a colon to separate a title from a subtitle.

   ▶ *A Writer's Tool: The Computer in Composition Instruction*

13d   Colon Problems

1. Do not use a colon when a period or other punctuation is more appropriate.

   ▶ We bought enough paper to last for several years. Paper for laser printers is less expensive when you buy it in quantity.

In this case, the two sentences are not sufficiently linked to justify using a colon.

2. Do not use a colon to separate a verb from its objects or complements.

▶ Three factors to consider when purchasing software are price, performance, and support.

or

▶ When purchasing software, consider these three factors: price, performance, and support.

14 The Apostrophe [']

The apostrophe has two different functions: it indicates possession (ownership), and it indicates omission of a letter or letters in contractions. Mastering a few standard rules for apostrophe use can help you detect and diagnose many common errors.

14a Indicating Possession

- With singular nouns, add -'s.

  ▶ The woman's briefcase was stolen.

- With plural nouns ending in -s, add an apostrophe only.

  ▶ The two countries' flags fly side by side.

- With plural nouns not ending in -s, add -'s.

  ▶ The children's bikes are in the driveway.

- With compound nouns, add -'s to the last element.

  ▶ My brother-in-law's hammering went on until dusk.

- With compound nouns indicating joint ownership, add -'s to the last element.

  ▶ Don and Marie's portrait hangs above their fireplace mantle.

- If there are two or more separate owners, add -'s to each noun.

  ▶ Our son's and daughter's dating habits are baffling.

- When a singular or plural name ends in *-s*, add either *-'s* or an apostrophe only.

  ▶ Charles's book is on the desk.

     or

  ▶ Charles' book is on the desk.

  ▶ The Douglas's house is in the country.

     or

  ▶ The Douglas' house is in the country.

Note: Convention calls for *Zeus'*, *Moses'*, and *Jesus'* as well as a single apostrophe with names like *Euripides* that are difficult to pronounce with an added syllable.

14b   Indicating Omission

In contractions.

  ▶ We're going home because I've got a cold.

Informally, in dates.

  ▶ The winter of '98 was surprisingly mild.

In standard or invented abbreviations.

  ▶ The story began on the front page, but the editor continued it on a later page, indicating the specific place with the words "cont'd, p. 3."

14c   Other Uses of the Apostrophe

Use *-'s* to form the plural of lowercase letters, abbreviations containing periods, and words used as examples of words.

  ▶ add *x*'s

  ▶ compare I.D.'s

  ▶ too many *no*'s

Note: It is acceptable to use *-s* only to form the plural of numbers and capital letters.

  ▶ 1960s

  ▶ the three Rs

A Quick Review of Possessive Apostrophe Rules

WITH SINGULAR NOUNS

- Add -'s to singular nouns not ending in -s.
  - ▶ the dog's collar
- Add -'s or a single apostrophe to singular nouns ending in -s.
  - ▶ my friend Bess's [or Bess'] mother

WITH PLURAL NOUNS

- Add a single apostrophe to plural nouns ending in -s.
  - ▶ the boys' clubhouse
- Add a single apostrophe or -'s to names.
  - ▶ the Santos' house
  - ▶ the Santos's house
- Add -'s to plural nouns not ending in -s.
  - ▶ our children's friends

WITH COMPOUND NOUNS

- In general, add -'s to the last element.
  - ▶ my son-in-law's wife
- Add -'s to the last element to show joint possession.
  - ▶ Abbott and Costello's comedy routines
- Add -'s to each element if there are two or more owners.
  - ▶ Roberta's and Carol's tastes were very different.

14d Common Errors with Apostrophes

Many people confuse the possessive form *its* ("belonging to it") with the contraction *it's* ("it is" or "it has"). Similarly, people sometimes confuse the possessive *your* ("belonging to you") with the contraction *you're* ("you are"). Whenever you use any of these forms, check your sentence to determine whether you have used the correct form. Read the sentence, substituting the full phrase (*you are, it has, it is*) for the contraction (*you're, it's*).

If the sentence does not make sense, then you know that you have to revise it.

▶ It's fur stood on end when the dog came into the room.

The sentence "It has fur stood on end" does not make sense.
Or you may have to substitute the contraction (or the uncontracted form of the word) for the possessive pronoun.

▶ It's been a long time since we met.

15 Quotation Marks [" "]

15a Quoting Exact Words

1. Use quotation marks to indicate someone's exact words, whether written, spoken, or thought.

   ▶ She said, "I'm happy that the course is almost over."

2. Use single quotation marks [' . . . '] to indicate a quotation within a quotation.

   ▶ She said, "I want you to remember that Frost's poem 'Out, Out' contains an allusion to Shakespeare's *Macbeth*."

3. Use indentation, instead of quotation marks, for quoting more than four typed lines of continuous prose or more than three printed lines. Shorter passages of poetry can also be indented for emphasis.

   ▶ The best part of her talk related to the uses of the Internet:

   > If students are going to benefit from their access to e-mail, then they have to learn how to do more than send and receive mail. They need to learn how to subscribe to lists, how to print text from the screen, and how to create groups of students to whom they can mail their text. (Hawisher 386)

15b Formal Definitions

Use quotation marks to indicate formal definitions or words not to be taken at face value.

▶ *Intrepid* means "bold" or "fearless."

▶ Then this "genius" forgot the keys.

Punctuating Direct Quotations

- When a direct quotation is followed by a "tag" (*he said*, *she said*, and so forth), place the punctuation inside the quotation marks.

  ▶ "Let's take a closer look," she said.

- When a direct quotation is interrupted by a tag, set off the tag with a pair of commas, inserting the first comma before the first close quotation mark.

  ▶ "May I," she asked, "take a closer look?"

- With a somewhat lengthy quotation, use a colon rather than a comma to introduce it.

  ▶ There are, according to Joseph Weizenbaum, severe limits on what we should ask of computers: "Since we do not have any ways of making computers wise, we ought not now to give computers tasks that demand wisdom."

- Semicolons are placed *outside* close quotation marks.

  ▶ You said, "The check is in the mail"; I can only respond, "Not in my mail."

- Colons are placed *outside* close quotation marks.

  ▶ According to Ann, these are John's "four basic food groups": burgers, pizza, fried chicken, and beer.

- Periods and commas are placed *inside* quotation marks.

  ▶ The speech ended with the words "I rest my case."

- When the quoted sentence ends in a question mark or an exclamation point, no comma is used.

  ▶ "May I take a closer look?" she asked.

- When the entire sentence is a question, a question mark is placed *outside* close quotation marks.

  ▶ What does the last line mean: "And miles to go before I sleep"?

- Quotations longer than four typed lines should be set off from the rest of your essay without quotation marks (unless they occur *within* the passage). Indent the quoted passage an additional half inch or five spaces on the left side only (total indentation: ten spaces).

15c Titles

Use quotation marks for titles of short works that are not part of a collection, individual items (stories, short poems, articles, songs, essays, and so forth) that usually appear in collections, episodes of radio and television shows, and subdivisions of a book.

▶ "A Rose for Emily" is a famous story by William Faulkner.

▶ "Saving Journalism" is an essay by Philip Meyer.

▶ My favorite *Simpsons* episode is "Selma's Choice."

▶ The chapter "The Creation of Sentences" was very helpful.

15d Quotations Within Sentences

Except for quotation marks, quotations integrated into sentences do not require additional punctuation.

▶ He knows that someday "things will even out."

Do not use quotation marks in describing what other people said (indirect discourse).

▶ His only reply was that someday he would get even.

16 Other Punctuation Marks

16a The Dash [—]

Most word-processing programs allow you to create the solid dash used in printed materials—called an em-dash. Otherwise, create a dash by typing two hyphens, one after the other, with no space before or after them.

The dash is used to emphasize a shift in tone or thought or to announce a list, a restatement, or an amplification—all matters that could be handled with other punctuation marks but with a slightly different effect. If used judiciously, dashes can help writers control the way their words are received by readers. Use a dash to get a reader's attention. A pair of dashes can be used in the middle of a sentence to emphasize—by setting off—an insertion in the middle of the sentence. Dashes are less formal than commas, but used in pairs they can serve a similar purpose.

▶ At the conference sat Roosevelt, Churchill, and Stalin—the leaders of the war against Hitler.

▶ He had practiced hard for the recital—did anyone realize how hard?—yet he was still nervous.

16b Parentheses [( )]

Parentheses are used to separate (or set aside) words or phrases from the rest of a sentence. Readers assume that the words between the parentheses are supplementary, intended to comment on or clarify a point. Occasionally, entire sentences are placed in parentheses to signal to a reader that additional information is being provided.

Use parentheses sparingly; substitute paired commas in those cases in which you want an additional comment to be more closely linked to the main flow of the sentence.

▶ Our local newspaper (at least it purports to be a newspaper) uncovered corruption.

1. Use parentheses to define terms that a reader cannot be expected to know.

   ▶ Several epidemiologists (scientists who study epidemics) were called in to assess the danger of rabies in the city.

2. Use parentheses to note a point that you would like a reader to consider, even though it is not essential to the gist of your text.

   ▶ A knowledge of computer programming (no longer thought to be an essential component of computer literacy) can enhance a technical writer's credibility with engineers.

3. Use parentheses to enclose in-text citations.

   ▶ *What Will Be* (Dertouzos) provides an exciting picture of technological change.

16c Ellipsis Points [. . .]

Ellipsis points are three equally spaced dots used to indicate that something in a passage is missing, such as part of a writer's exact words in a quotation. Note that you need one space after each dot.

Use ellipsis points in a documented paper when you want to omit material from a long quotation. Use ellipsis points only in the middle of a quote and at the end. Take care not to distort the meaning of the original text through your use of ellipsis points: if the text says that "Movie X was technically flawed and not enjoyable," do not write, "Movie X was . . . enjoyable."

▶ I disagree with the argument that the "students of the twenty-first century . . . will rarely use pencil and paper."

Use of ellipsis points also indicates that something is unfinished; it is acceptable—if it is not overused—in informal writing. In the example below, the first period concludes the sentence (without a space); it is then followed by the three ellipsis points with a space between each.

▶ And that's the way things went for me. . . .

16d Square Brackets [ ]

Square brackets are used to enclose words that you, as editor, have inserted into a quote for the purpose of clarity or of producing a grammatically correct sentence.

▶ Then the speaker concluded: "Our efforts at such [campaign financing] reforms have never appeared more promising."

Brackets are also used around parenthetical material within parentheses.

▶ These nudes are clearly Rubenesque (after the Flemish painter Peter Paul Rubens [1577–1640]).

The Latin term *sic* ("thus") is traditionally used inside brackets to indicate an obvious error in the original source, although at times it is more helpful just to give the correction inside the brackets.

▶ The sign said: This sail [*sic*] ends tomorrow.

16e The Slash [/]

The slash is sometimes used to indicate alternative words of equal weight.

▶ Schools are offering more pass/fail courses.

▶ Each student has his/her own computer.

Do not use *his/her* or *he/she* constructions routinely, however, since they generally distract your readers. To avoid referring to the generic pronoun *he*, rewrite the above sentence, using the plural. (See section 7e, page 38.)

▶ All of the students have their own computers.

A slash is also used to indicate lines of poetry when they are not indented, but are run into the text. Be sure to put a space before and after the slash.

▶ I've often wondered what Robert Frost meant by repeating the last two lines of "Stopping by Woods on a Snowy Evening": "And miles to go before I sleep, / And miles to go before I sleep."

Mechanics

17 Capitalization

Academic writing tasks require correct use of capital letters. Use these guidelines, and consult a dictionary when you have questions.

17a   The First Word in a Sentence

The first word in a sentence must be capitalized. If you quote a complete sentence, you must capitalize the first word in the quotation.

> ▶ In Roger Ebert's opinion, "Movie critics aren't supposed to give away the plots of thrillers."

17b   Proper Nouns and Modifiers Derived from Them

A proper noun is a noun that names a specific person, place, or thing. Capitalize all proper nouns.

> ▶ *President Siegel* asked students to work on flood-relief efforts.

> ▶ Parts of *Colorado* suffered flooding in 1997.

> ▶ *Canada* was settled by both the English and the French.

> ▶ The *Kennesaw State Student Government Association* established a flood-relief committee.

Modifiers derived from proper nouns are usually capitalized.

> ▶ Delegates from twenty *African* countries met at the United Nations.

"African" is a modifier created by adding -*n* to the proper noun.

▶ The *Canadian* parliament is modeled on parliament structures in place in Great Britain.

17c Titles of Works

Capitalize the first and last words in a title and all other words except conjunctions, articles, and prepositions of four letters or less.

▶ *Pride and Prejudice*

▶ *Leaves of Grass*

▶ "Battle Hymn of the Republic"

17d Personal Titles

1. Titles used before personal names must be capitalized.

   ▶ My optometrist is *Dr.* Ross.

   ▶ Former *President* Richard Nixon's record was tarnished by the Watergate incident.

   ▶ I'll always remember *Aunt* Maria.

   However, titles used after personal names are usually lowercase.

   ▶ Hillary Clinton, the Democratic *senator* from New York

2. Titles that refer to a high position may be capitalized even when they are used without the name of the person holding that title.

   ▶ the Pope

   ▶ the President

   ▶ the Director

17e Other Capitalization Rules

THE FIRST WORD IN LINES OF POETRY   Capitalize the first word in each line of a poem, whether or not the poetic line forms a complete sentence, unless the author has intentionally chosen not to capitalize the words.

▶ Whose woods these are I think I know

▶ anyone lived in a pretty how town

In the second example, "anyone" should not be capitalized because E. E. Cummings, the author, did not capitalize this line, the first line of his poem "anyone lived in a pretty how town."

SPECIFIC SCHOOL OR COLLEGE COURSES   Capitalize the specific title of a course. Do not capitalize the names of courses if you are referring to them generally rather than specifically, except for language courses.

▶ My *art* course is *Art 301*. My *French* course is *French 350*.

▶ I'm taking two *English* courses: *American Literature* and *Advanced Composition*.

17f Capitalization Errors

Do not capitalize the following:

1. The words *a*, *an*, and *the* when used with proper nouns

   ▶ a Democrat

   ▶ the *New Yorker*

2. The seasons of the year

   ▶ the fall semester

3. Decades

   ▶ the twenties

CHECKLIST 13   **A Quick Review of Capitalization Rules**

ALWAYS CAPITALIZE
● the first word in a sentence.
● all proper nouns.
● titles used before personal names.
● the specific title of a course.

USUALLY CAPITALIZE
● modifiers derived from proper nouns.
● the first word in a line of poetry.

18 Italics, Abbreviations, Numbers

18a Italics for Titles of Full-Length Works

Italicize or underline titles of full-length works, including books, periodicals, films, TV or radio shows, works of visual art, plays, poems published separately as books, and so forth.

▶ *Desperate Housewives*

▶ the *Washington Post*

▶ Picasso's *Guernica*

Use quotation marks to note shorter works such as magazine or newspaper articles, short stories, episodes of TV shows, and so on.

▶ The *Family Guy* episode "Road to Rhode Island" is Amanda's favorite.

▶ The article "How to Help Your Child Learn to Read," published in the *Transcript*, is invaluable.

18b Other Rules for Italics

LETTERS OR WORDS REFERRED TO AS OBJECTS   Italicize or underline letters or words used as letters or words.

▶ Remember to cross that *t* and to dot that *i*.

▶ It seems as if every other word she uses is either *like* or *you know*.

TERMS ABOUT TO BE FORMALLY DEFINED   Italicize or underline terms if you are about to define them. Remember to put the definition in quotation marks.

▶ The verb *vex* means "to puzzle."

NAMES OF SHIPS AND VEHICLES   Italicize or underline the names of ships and vehicles.

▶ Lindbergh's *Spirit of St. Louis* now hangs in the Smithsonian.

FOREIGN WORDS AND PHRASES   Italicize or underline foreign words and phrases not yet considered part of English, and set off their translation (if given) with quotation marks.

Punctuating Titles

- Enclose in quotation marks titles of short works—poems, short stories, articles, songs, essays, episodes of radio and television shows, and subdivisions of a book.

  ▶ "When Lilacs Last in the Dooryard Bloom'd" is a poem about the death of Abraham Lincoln.

- Italicize (or underline) titles of large works such as books, periodicals, films, television or radio shows, works of visual art, plays, poems published separately as books.

  ▶ *Leaves of Grass* is probably Whitman's most widely circulated collection of poetry.

- Capitalize the first word, the last word, and all other words in a title *except* coordinating conjunctions, articles (*a, an, the*), and prepositions of four letters or less.

  ▶ *Death of a Salesman*

  ▶ *Two Years Before the Mast*

  ▶ *The Norton Field Guide to Writing*

  ▶ *The Egg and I*

▶ Visitors to Quebec should take time to review their French—in particular, traffic signs such as *Arrête* ("Stop").

18c Abbreviations

Use abbreviations sparingly and only when you are sure your readers will understand what you are referring to. Increasingly, abbreviations are accepted as alternate forms of longer terms, and, thus, they are written without spaces or periods between the letters. This practice is especially common when abbreviations are composed of all capital letters (such as acronyms), capital-letter abbreviations of technical terms (URL for Uniform Resource Locater), and names of agencies (FBI) and organizations (NATO).

To use a less widely known abbreviation throughout a paper, write out the full name for your first reference and immediately follow it with its abbreviation in parentheses.

▶ The Federal Trade Commission (FTC) was established in 1914.

APPROPRIATE ABBREVIATIONS

1. Titles used before and after names are appropriate and can be used freely.

   ▶ Mr., Ms., Rev., Jr., MBA

   Do not use titles when you are citing. Say, "As Kennedy says," not "As Dr. Kennedy says."

2. Common abbreviations of time and measurement are acceptable and can be used freely.

   ▶ B.C.E. or BCE

   ▶ C.E. or CE

   ▶ a.m. or A.M.

   ▶ 3 p.m. or 3 P.M.

   ▶ no. (for *number*, when followed by a specific figure)

3. Use capital letters for common acronyms. Acronyms of three letters or more are customarily written without periods.

   ▶ IBM, YMCA, PBS

INAPPROPRIATE ABBREVIATIONS Do not abbreviate the following:

1. Personal names

   ▶ ~~Steve~~ Stephen Jones led the investigation.

2. Days of the week, months of the year, and holidays

   ▶ Classes do not meet on ~~Dec.~~ December 25.

3. Names of academic subjects

   ▶ I am taking ~~econ, poli sci,~~ economics, political science, and English.

4. Names of most states and countries (*Washington, D.C.,* and the *USA* being exceptions) in an academic paper

   ▶ She lives in ~~PA~~ Pennsylvania during the summer.

5. Divisions of a written text (like chapter and page)

   ▶ The poem is cited in ~~chap. one~~ chapter 1 on ~~p.~~ page 3.

18d Numbers

IN GENERAL Spell out numbers of one or two words up to ninety-nine, unless there are several numbers within a sentence. For numbers requiring three or more words, use numerals.

▶ twenty

▶ 120

▶ fifty-five

▶ Enrollment figures show that we have 910 returning freshman, 100 transfer students, and 30 graduate students.

The numbers "100" and "30" are not spelled out because there are several numbers in this sentence.

AT THE BEGINNING OF SENTENCES If a sentence begins with a number, either spell out the number or, better, reword the sentence.

▶ ~~150~~ *One hundred fifty* species of water lily are found in the pond.

or

▶ The pond is home to 150 species of water lily.

USED FOR CLARITY Use numbers, even in nontechnical writing, to specify exactness in such things as pages and divisions of texts (*page 12*), addresses (*1600 Pennsylvania Avenue*), dates (*May 22, 1978*), time (*9:45 a.m.*), and measurements (*95 percent*). In dealing with the many special cases, remember to be consistent within your own paper.

19 The Hyphen and Spelling

19a The Hyphen [-]

A hyphen is used to form compound adjectives or compound nouns and with words formed by adding a capital letter.

▶ in-laws, H-bomb

Use a hyphen to show that two or more words are being used as a single adjective before a noun. But when a compound adjective follows a noun, the hyphen is often not used.

▶ a USB-ready computer

▶ a computer that is USB ready

Use a hyphen to prevent misreading and awkward constructions.

▶ a little-used printer

▶ a re-covered book

Use a hyphen with certain prefixes.

▶ self-sacrifice

▶ ex-president

▶ all-inclusive

Note that some compound words (like *real estate*) are written as two words, others (like *manic-depressive*) are hyphenated, while still others (like *fainthearted*) are one word. It is best to rely on a dictionary or spelling checker.

Use a hyphen when writing out compound numbers and fractions.

▶ One-fourth of the class graduated with honors.

▶ Numbers from twenty-one to ninety-nine should be hyphenated.

If you choose to divide a word at the end of a line, be sure to hyphenate it between syllables. Check a dictionary whenever you are unsure of how to divide a word.

Do not hyphenate the last word of a line; transpose the entire word to the last line.

If part of a compound term falls at the end of the line, hyphenate between words, not between syllables.

19b Spelling Rules

Correct spelling is important on final drafts. Even if you are a good speller, be sure to run the spelling checker before submitting your paper to either your peers or your teacher. Proofread your paper carefully, remembering to see if you have used words such as *their* and *there* correctly, for a spelling checker often cannot tell if you have used the wrong word. Finally, make frequent use of your dictionary.

Here are a few spelling pointers to keep in mind:

1. Use *i* before *e* except after *c* or when sounding like *ay* as in *neighbor* or *weigh*.

   ▶ believe, receive, sleigh

   EXCEPTIONS   either, seize, height, foreign, weird

2. Words that end in a silent -*e* usually drop the -*e* when a suffix is added if the suffix begins with a vowel. If the suffix begins with a consonant, however, retain the final -*e*.

   ▶ believe, believable; achieve, achievement

   EXCEPTIONS acknowledgment, judgment, changeable, argument

3. The root word doesn't change if it is preceded by a prefix.

   ▶ misshapen, disbelief, excommunicate

4. British and American spellings differ for some words.

   ▶ theater (American), theatre (British)

   ▶ honor (American), honour (British)

   ▶ realize (American), realise (British)

   ▶ canceled (American), cancelled (British)

   In your paper, use American spelling throughout, except when you are quoting from British sources, in which case you must retain the spellings of the original source.

Refer to the rules below when forming plurals:

1. Form the plural of most nouns by adding -*s* to the noun. Add an -*es* to nouns that end in -*ch*, -*s*, -*sh*, and -*x*.

   ▶ sailboat, sailboats; church, churches

2. Form the plural of most words that end in -*y* by changing the -*y* to *i* and adding -*es*, except when the -*y* is preceded by a vowel. Just add -*s* to proper names ending in -*y*.

   ▶ variety, varieties; donkey, donkeys; Mary, Marys

3. Form the plural of most words ending in -*o* by adding -*s*. However, if the -*o* is preceded by a consonant, add -*es*.

   ▶ radio, radios; potato, potatoes

4. Add an -*s* to the main word of a hyphenated compound word to form its plural.

   ▶ mothers-in-law, jacks-of-all-trade

5. Words that are derived from other languages sometimes retain the plural of the original language.

► chateau, chateaux; lied, lieder

19c Improving Your Spelling

Determine how you can best improve your spelling. Different people learn spelling in different ways. Some find that saying a word out loud and then writing it down helps. Others find that doing a spell check and then mentally sounding out the correct word before directing the computer to insert the word can help. Still other people like to develop mnemonic devices, or memory aids, such as these: *principal* ends in *-pal* because the princi*pal* is your *pal*; *independent* has *depend* in it.

One suggestion is to keep a log of your frequently misspelled words. Do not include difficult words with which everyone has trouble. Rather, start with basic words that you have trouble spelling. Note any patterns in the errors you make.

Note: Many word-processing programs, including Microsoft® Word, allow you to add words to a customized dictionary as you run the spelling checker.

19d Tracking Your Spelling Demons

All word processors have sophisticated, helpful, but imperfect spelling checkers. Such programs will catch many misspellings and typos but may not detect instances in which you have used the wrong word—for example, *there* instead of *their*. Keep a file of your spelling demons. As the final step for any writing project, use the *Find* function in your word processor to find these troublesome words in the context of your work.

19e Frequently Misspelled Words

You may find it helpful to memorize a list of frequently misspelled words, such as the following:

absence	achievement	aggravate	analyze
academic	acknowledge	all right	answer
accidentally	acquaintance	a lot	apparently
accommodate	acquire	altogether	appearance
accomplish	across	amateur	appropriate
accumulate	address	among	argument

arithmetic
arrangement
ascend
athlete
athletics
attendance
audience
basically
beginning
believe
benefited
Britain
bureau
business
cafeteria
calendar
candidate
cemetery
changeable
characteristic
chosen
column
commitment
committed
committee
comparative
competitive
conceivable
conference
conferred
conqueror
conscience
conscientious
conscious
courteous
criticism
criticize
curiosity
dealt
decision
definitely
descendant
describe
description
despair

desperate
develop
dictionary
disappear
disappoint
disastrous
dissatisfied
eighth
eligible
embarrass
eminent
emphasize
entirely
environment
equivalent
especially
exaggerated
exhaust
existence
experience
extraordinary
extremely
familiar
fascinate
February
foreign
forty
fourth
friend
government
grammar
guard
guidance
harass
height
humorous
illiterate
immediately
incredible
indefinitely
indispensable
inevitable
infinite
intelligence
interesting

irrelevant
irresistible
knowledge
laboratory
legitimate
license
lightning
loneliness
maintenance
maneuver
mathematics
mischievous
necessary
noticeable
occasion
occasionally
occur
occurred
occurrence
optimistic
original
outrageous
pamphlet
parallel
particularly
pastime
performance
permissible
perseverance
perspiration
phenomenon
physically
picnicking
playwright
politics
practically
precede
precedence
preference
preferred
prejudice
primitive
privilege
probably
proceed

professor
prominent
pronunciation
quiet
quite
receive
recommend
reference
referred
religion
repetition
restaurant
rhythmical
rhythm
roommate
schedule
secretary
seize
separate
sergeant
several
siege
similar
sincerely
sophomore
subtly
succeed
surprise
temperature
thorough
tragedy
transferred
truly
unnecessarily
until
usually
vacuum
vengeance
villain
weird
whether
writing

INDEX

CONTENTS